MULTICULTURAL BIOGRAPHIES COLLECTION

ASIAN AMERICAN BIOGRAPHIES

GLOBE FEARON

EDUCATIONAL PUBLISHER

PARAMUS, NEW JERSEY

Paramount Publishing

Executive Editor: Virginia Seeley
Senior Editor: Barbara Levadi
Project Editor: Lynn W. Kloss
Production Editor: June E. Bodansky
Editorial Developer: Book Production Systems, Inc.
Art Director: Nancy Sharkey
Production Manager: Penny Gibson
Production Coordinator: Nicole Cypher
Cover and Interior Design: B B & K Design, Inc.
Cover Illustration: Jane Sterrett
Marketing Managers: Elmer Ildefonso, Sandra Hutchison
Photo Research: Jenifer Hixson, Holly Price
Electronic Page Production: Siren Design

Printed in the United States of America.   2 3 4 5 6 7 8 9 10 97 96 95

ISBN: 0-835-90617-5

GLOBE FEARON
EDUCATIONAL PUBLISHER
PARAMUS, NEW JERSEY

Paramount Publishing

CONTENTS

You have probably read many biographies since you have been in school. Because no biography can describe everything about a person, a biographer usually writes with a focus, or a theme of the subject's life, in mind. A collection of biographies also has a focus, so that if you wanted to learn, for example, about sports figures or famous scientists, you could quickly find a book that tells about people in these fields.

The biographies presented in this book introduce you to 21 people whose cultural backgrounds are Asian. The book explores their heritages and how these heritages influenced their lives. It also reveals how these people became successful in their careers.

The book is divided into four units. Each unit features the life stories of several people whose careers are related to subjects you study in school. The map of Asia on page 1 shows you the locations of places mentioned in the biographies.

In addition, a directory of career resources and a bibliography are located at the back of the book. These resources suggest books, magazines, and agencies that can tell you more about the people and careers discussed.

As you read, think about the different cultural heritages that are part of the description *Asian American*. Notice, too, that even though people around the world have different traditions, all cultures have similarities. By recognizing our similarities and respecting our differences, we can come to know and understand one another.

ACKNOWLEDGMENTS

p. 4:(top) photo © Robert Foothorap, courtesy G.P. Putnam's Sons; (bottom) courtesy Richard Kim; **p. 5**:(top) B.D. Wong; (center) courtesy W.W. Norton & Company, Inc; (bottom) courtesy M. J. Perna; **p. 6**: © Robert Foothorap; **p. 7**: © Robert Foothorap, courtesy G. Putnam's Sons; **p. 15,16**: courtesy Richard Kim; **p. 24**: © 1993 Martha Swope; **p. 25**: Courtesy David Henry Hwang; **p. 33,34**: courtesy W.W. Norton & Company, Inc; **p. 42,43**: courtesy M. J. Perna; **p. 60**:(top) © Arthur Tress; (bottom) © Richard Howard; **p. 61**:(top) courtesy Greenwillow Publishing; (center) © Joe McNally/CBS Photo; (bottom) Reuters/Betmann; **p. 62**: UPI/Bettmann; **p. 63**: © Arthur Tress; **p. 71**: © Adam Stoltzman; **p. 72**: © Richard Howard; **p. 82**: courtesy Greenwillow Publishing; **p. 90**: © Tony Esparza/CBS Photo; **p. 91**: © Joe McNally/CBS Photo; **p. 99**: UPI/Bettmann; **p. 100**: Reuters/Bettmann; **p. 116**:(top) Photofest; (bottom) courtesy ICM Artists; **p. 117**:(top) David Madison © duomo; (center) Shooting Star; (bottom) courtesy Columbia Artists Management; **p. 118,119**: Shooting Star; **p. 127**: © Walter H. Scott; **p. 128**: courtesy ICM Artists; **p. 136**: © Rick Rickman/duomo; **p. 137**: David Madison © duomo; **p. 146,147**: © Steve Ellison, Shooting Star; **p. 155**: courtesy Columbia Artists Management Inc.; **p. 156**: courtesy ICM Artists; **p. 172**:(top) courtesy Wang Labs, Inc.; (bottom) courtesy Congressional Office of Patsy Takemoto Mink; **p. 173**:(top right) UPI/Bettmann; (top left) courtesy Constance Tom Noguchi; (bottom right) UPI/Bettmann; (bottom left) courtesy Juan Montero; **p. 174,175**: courtesy Wang Labs, Inc; **p. 183**: UPI/Bettmann; **p. 184**: courtesy Congressional Office of Patsy Takemoto Mink; **p. 192,193**: UPI/Bettmann; **p. 200,201**: courtesy Constance Tom Noguchi; **p. 209,210:** UPI/Bettmann; **p. 217,218:** courtesy Juan Montero.

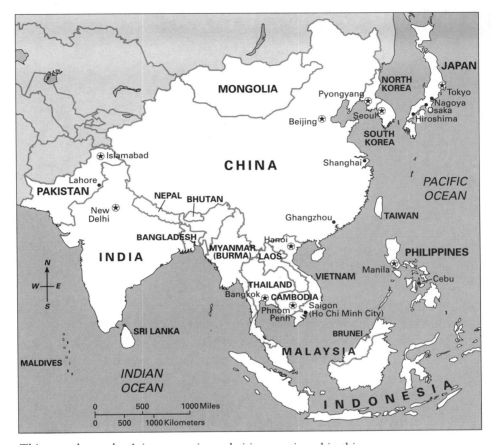

This map shows the Asian countries and cities mentioned in this book.

INTRODUCTION

A biography is a portrait of a person that is presented in words rather than pictures. Details about historical events, personal tragedies and successes, family traits and cultural traditions, and individual talents are often included to help the reader "get to know" the subject.

No biography can tell everything about a person. To try to tell everything would mean that a biographer would write either an enormous book with a great deal of detail about unimportant events or a book that covers every event, even important ones, very quickly. Biographers, then, must choose the areas they wish to explore so that they will help the reader understand at least part of a person's life fully.

This book introduces you to 21 Asian Americans. Their biographies focus on three areas of their lives: childhood experiences, cultural heritage, and career goals. Although they all have Asian heritage, each life story is unique. As you read, you will notice similarities among them, but you will also find that each has his or her own definition of success and of what it means to be an Asian American.

Childhood experiences What a person experiences as a child often affects the type of person he or she becomes. Particularly exciting or unhappy times can have a major impact. For example, Indian American writer Ved Mehta lost his sight at the age of 3. He says his blindness is one reason he became a writer. He uses writing to explore the world and to relieve the loneliness he often feels.

Some of the people you will read about do not discuss much about their childhood experiences. For them, achievements later in life are more important.

Cultural heritage Culture includes language, religion, and family structure. It is expressed through people's customs, food and clothing, and behavior. Culture is also expressed through art, music, and writing. Some of the Asian Americans you will read about have been shaped by their heritage. For example, inventor

An Wang was strongly influenced by the lessons his grandmother taught him about Chinese philosophy.

For others, culture did not become important until adulthood. TV reporter Connie Chung came to understand her heritage only after she achieved success in the United States and visited China, the homeland of her parents.

Career goals A person's goals, struggles, and successes also reveal a great deal about him or her. Some of these biographies tell of commitments to career goals at a very young age. Musician Myung-Whun Chung and ice skater Kristi Yamaguchi began to perform before the age of 5. In the same way, medical doctor Juan Montero knew from a very young age that he wanted to be a doctor.

Other Asian Americans presented here changed their career goals after they became adults. For example, illustrator José Aruego left the legal profession and politician Patsy Mink left the field of medicine to pursue new careers.

Personal challenges Many of the people you will read about have encountered prejudice because they "looked different." Some, like Yoshiko Uchida, were forced to live in internment camps because of their cultural background.

Several people came to the United States because their homeland had been torn apart by war. Actors Dustin Nguyen from Vietnam and Haing Ngor from Cambodia are examples. Barriers to success in a new country included having to learn a new language and customs, find a job, and replace possessions they were forced to leave behind.

Others, such as playwright David Henry Hwang, grew up in the United States under comfortable conditions. For these people, barriers have come from within, too, in the form of questions about how their Asian and American heritages fit together.

Biographies tell a person's life story, but they can also help the reader learn more about himself or herself. As you read, think about these questions: What do you admire about these people? With which points of view do you agree or disagree? Which people and careers do you want to learn more about? In short, what do your reactions to these biographies tell you about yourself?

ASIAN AMERICANS IN LITERATURE AND DRAMA

In this unit, you will read about some Asian American writers. Although they have all had critical and popular success and been influenced by their heritages, their writings and life stories are quite different. As you read this unit, think about some of the qualities that make these writers different from each other. Think also about how each person's cultural heritage and background influenced that writer's life and work.

Amy Tan, a Chinese American, has asked herself, "How can you keep your Chinese face and keep your American face and not hide anything and not be dishonest."

The Korean American writer **Richard E. Kim** said, "I had wanted to write about my grandfather's fate. I tried to get inside his mind . . . and then the novel took its own shape and course. I seemed to have tried to define myself in it."

David Henry Hwang (WAHNG), a Chinese American playwright, says, "I knew I was Chinese, but growing up it never occurred to me that that should [make me different] in any way. I thought it was a minor detail, like having red hair."

The Indian American writer **Ved Mehta** (VEHD MAY-tuh) spoke of his blindness and his writing: "Partly I write because of blindness, because of the heightened sense of loneliness that many intelligent blind people feel."

"I find bits and pieces of my child self turning up in my writing," observed **Yoshiko Uchida** (yoh-SHEE-koh oo-CHEE-dah), a Japanese American. Her writing, she has said, tries to "preserve the magic as well as the joy and sadness of certain moments in my life."

As you read this unit, think about how each person's writing grew out of his or her experiences. Think, too, about how writing has affected the way each person views the world.

AMY TAN

Amy Tan, Chinese American writer, reads in her home. Among the
books that influenced Tan's choice of career was *Love Medicine* by
Louise Erdrich, a Native American writer.

Amy Tan did not plan to become a writer. She planned to be a doctor. After all, that was what her parents wanted. John and Daisy Tan, who had emigrated[1] to the United States from China in the late 1940s, faced many hardships in giving Amy and her two brothers a better life. They thought that Amy should become a neurosurgeon.[2] They also wanted her to play the piano. As Amy later said, "From the age of six I was led to believe that I would grow up to be a neurosurgeon by trade and a concert pianist by hobby."

Amy, however, had her own dreams. Born in Oakland, California, in 1952, she did not want to be bound by her parents' expectations. In fact, throughout much of her early life, she wanted nothing to do with her Chinese heritage. She wanted to assimilate[3] into U.S. culture. "There is this myth[4] that America is a melting pot," she has said, "but what happens in assimilation is that we end up deliberately choosing the American things—hot dogs and apple pie—and ignoring the Chinese offerings."

Amy did not use her Chinese name, *An-mei*, which means *blessing from America*. Instead, she became *Amy*, a name that carried no hint of her background. She wished she could also get rid of her Chinese looks. At one point she slept with a clothespin on her nose, hoping to make her nose look thinner and less

---

1. **emigrated** (EHM-uh-grayt-uhd) *v.* left one country or region to settle in another
2. **neurosurgeon** (noo-roh-SER-juhn) *n.* a doctor who operates on the brain and other parts of the nervous system
3. **assimilate** (uh-SIHM-uh-layt) *v.* to absorb groups of different cultures into the main culture
4. **myth** (MIHTH) *n.* usually, a traditional story that attempts to explain nature or people; here, it means something that is not true

"Chinese." She also felt that her parents did not understand her. "When I was growing up, I blamed everything on the fact that my mother was Chinese while I thought of myself as totally American."

Amy dreamed of becoming a writer, but the idea seemed "as preposterous[5] as a Chinese girl dreaming of becoming president of the United States." She needed a career that would allow her to earn a large amount of money so that her family would be proud of her. She would then be able to provide for her parents as they grew old. "That's really what success is about in Chinese families,—" she said, "it's not success for yourself, it's success so you can take care of your family." (See **Did You Know?** on page 11 for more information on Chinese attitudes about the family.)

In 1967, when Amy was 15, tragedy struck the Tans. Amy's father and her 16-year-old brother Peter both developed brain tumors and died. Then her mother made the shocking announcement that Amy was not her only daughter. Daisy had been married in China and had had three daughters. She explained that her first husband had treated her badly and that she had divorced him. Upon divorce, Chinese courts at that time automatically gave custody of the children to their father.

Amy was stunned to learn of her mother's past. She also felt threatened by her three half sisters. She imagined these girls as beautiful, talented, loving daughters—daughters who were very different from her. Amy thought of all the times she had fought with her mother. Suddenly Amy felt she was the "wicked daughter."

Daisy decided to take Amy and 13-year-old John, Jr., to live in Switzerland for one year. After the family moved back to California, Daisy decided that Amy would go to Linfield College in McMinnville, Oregon, to prepare for medical school. Within a year, though, Amy met and fell in love with Louis DeMattei. When Lou moved to California to attend San Jose State University, Amy went with him. She also stopped preparing for

---

5. **preposterous** (prih-PAHS-tuhr-uhs) *adj.* ridiculous

medical school and decided to study English literature instead.

Daisy Tan was furious. She could not understand why her daughter would throw away the family's longstanding plans. "I remember her saying something about how disappointed my father would be," Amy later recalled. "Chinese parents express their love by guiding their children in the right direction, and I'd ignored my parents' wisdom."

Amy knew how her mother felt. But she did not let that stop her. Instead, Amy earned her bachelor's degree in English and her master's degree in linguistics[6] in 1974. In 1974, she also married Lou DeMattei.

Although she now had a background in English, Amy still did not see herself as a writer. Then one day her boss told her that writing was her "worst skill" and that she should focus on her strong math abilities. Determined to prove him wrong, she started her writing career one week later.

At first, she wrote speeches for businesspeople. Because she still felt uncomfortable about her Chinese roots, she wrote under the name May Brown. By 1983, she was writing speeches and papers for companies such as IBM and Apple. This work made her a great deal of money, allowing her to buy her mother a house. "My mother started feeling that maybe I was doing okay for myself."

Then Amy began reading fiction. One of the books she read was *Love Medicine* by Louise Erdrich, a Native American writer from the Chippewa nation. As she later said, "What struck me about Erdrich was that her voice was unique."

Amy started thinking that she, too, might have a unique voice. Perhaps her experiences as a Chinese American would serve her well as a writer. Writing about her experiences might help her understand her own, and Daisy's, feelings.

In 1985, Amy wrote her first short story. It was exciting to feel her childhood dream finally coming true. She also found an agent, someone who would try to sell her writing to publishers.

---

6. **linguistics** (lihng-GWIHS-tihks) *n. pl.* the study of language

In 1986, Amy turned her attention to her mother. Daisy was admitted to the hospital with heart problems. Amy was unhappy that she and her mother still did not understand each other. "I decided that if my mother was okay, I'd get to know her." Amy decided on a bold action: She would take her mother to China. Together they would visit the daughters Daisy had left behind so many years earlier.

The following year, Amy and Daisy went to China. The trip changed Amy's life forever. "When my feet touched China, I became Chinese," she said. "There was something about this country that I belonged to. I found something about myself that I never knew was there." At last Amy felt she understood how her Chinese heritage fit into her life. She was "finally able to say, 'I'm both Chinese and American.'"

This feeling deepened when Amy met her half sisters, who were not the perfect daughters she had imagined. They were real people and they were her family. "The way they smiled, the way they held their hands, all those things connected me. I had family in China. I belonged."

When Amy returned to California, more good news awaited her. Her agent had found a publisher for Amy's stories. The publisher, G.P. Putnam's Sons, wanted to turn the stories into a book and send Amy a check for $50,000.

Stunned by this news, Amy quit her business writing and threw all her energies into the 16 stories that would make up the book. The stories told of four Chinese American girls and their immigrant Chinese mothers. For Amy, writing these stories meant exploring what it was to be Chinese American. "I think what I was trying to find was how can you have the best of both worlds; how can you keep your Chinese face and keep your American face and not hide anything and not be dishonest."

Her book *The Joy Luck Club*, which was published in March 1989, soon became a bestseller. Readers were moved by the tales of her characters and understood her descriptions of mother-daughter conflicts.

Clearly, Amy had become a success. She had earned more wealth and fame than even her mother had imagined for her. Amy had not followed the route laid out by John and Daisy Tan. But she had indeed reached the top of a respected profession.

In 1991, Amy published her second successful book, *The Kitchen God's Wife*. This book also explored her Chinese heritage, but in a more personal way. She based the book on the life story of Daisy Tan. "The most terrible things that happened [in the book] happened to my mother," Amy told one reporter. "And I left out things that were even worse."

With the writing of *The Joy Luck Club* and *The Kitchen God's Wife*, Amy Tan proved that she was indeed the product of both China and the United States. She showed everyone—including herself—that this is a wonderfully rich heritage. It is not always easy to be Chinese American. But as Amy Tan showed, the struggle to bridge the two worlds brings many rewards.

Did You Know? *Throughout history, the family in China has been considered more important than the individual. Traditionally, the Chinese family consisted of a father and a mother, all their sons, their unmarried daughters, and their sons' wives and children. Although many changes have occurred in China since the Communists took power in 1949, family ties remain strong. For example, families are still required, both by law and by tradition, to support their older and disabled members. Unlike people from the United States, who value individual success, Chinese households measure their wealth by combining the income of the entire family.*

AFTER YOU READ

EXPLORING YOUR RESPONSES

1. Amy says that the idea of a Chinese girl dreaming of becoming President is "preposterous." Do you think it would be preposterous for you or someone you know to become President? Why or why not?

2. Amy felt that her Chinese heritage made her an "outsider." How might you help another person feel more at home in a new situation?

3. Amy's parents felt that success means "You can take care of your family." What do you think success means?

4. Amy hid her Chinese heritage by using false names. Do you think hiding their heritage helps people succeed today? Why or why not?

5. When Amy's boss told her that writing was her worst skill, she decided to prove him wrong. Has anyone ever tried to discourage you from doing something you wanted to do? How did you prove that person wrong?

UNDERSTANDING WORDS IN CONTEXT

Read the following sentences from the biography. Think about what each underlined word means. In your notebook, write what the word means as it is used in the sentence.

1. John and Daisy Tan . . . had emigrated to the United States from China in the late 1940s.

2. In fact, throughout much of her early life, [Amy] wanted nothing to do with her Chinese heritage. She wanted to assimilate into U.S. culture.

3. "There is this myth that America is a melting pot," she has said, "but what happens in assimilation is that we end up deliberately choosing the American things–hot dogs and apple pie–and ignoring the Chinese offerings."

4. Amy dreamed of becoming a writer, but the idea seemed "as <u>preposterous</u> as a Chinese girl dreaming of becoming president of the United States."

5. She planned to be a doctor. After all, that was what her parents wanted. John and Daisy Tan . . . thought that Amy should become a <u>neurosurgeon</u>.

RECALLING DETAILS

1. Why did Amy begin writing speeches for businesspeople?
2. Who was May Brown? Why did Amy create her?
3. What was Amy's reaction after she read Louise Erdrich's *Love Medicine*?
4. What was Amy's first reaction when she set foot on Chinese soil?
5. What steps did Amy take to become a novelist?

UNDERSTANDING INFERENCES

In your notebook, write two or three sentences from the story that support each of the following inferences.

1. John and Daisy Tan's Chinese heritage influenced the way they raised Amy.
2. Daisy did not have a happy life in China.
3. Amy liked to make her own decisions.
4. Amy learned to value her Chinese heritage.
5. Daisy decided that Amy had made a good choice in her career.

INTERPRETING WHAT YOU HAVE READ

1. Amy's parents named her *An-mei,* which means *blessing from America.* What does this tell you about Daisy and John's feelings about the United States?

2. Why do you think Amy imagined her sisters to be beautiful, talented, and loving?

3. Why do you think reading Louise Erdrich's book had such a strong influence on Amy?

4. How do you think Amy's feelings toward her mother changed after their trip to China?

5. Why did Amy's feelings about her Chinese heritage change?

ANALYZING QUOTATIONS

Read the following quotation from the biography and answer the questions below.

> *"When my feet touched China, I became Chinese. There was something about this country that I belonged to. I found something about myself that I never knew was there."*

1. Why do you think visiting China made such a change in the way Amy looked at herself and her heritage?

2. What other experiences do you think could stir such strong feelings about a person's heritage?

3. If you could do one thing that would help you understand your own heritage, what would it be and why?

THINKING CRITICALLY

1. Why do you think Amy chose to be a writer?

2. In what ways might Amy's career path have been different if her parents had supported her writing from the beginning?

3. Amy said, "There is this myth that America is a melting pot." Do you agree or disagree with her? Why?

4. Amy's role model was the Chippewa writer Louise Erdrich. Who are your role models and why did you choose them?

5. How was Amy's parents' definition of success different from that of other parents you know?

RICHARD E. KIM

Richard Kim, Korean American writer, draws upon his personal
experiences and cultural heritage in his fiction. Kim's book *Lost
Names: Scenes from a Boyhood in Japanese-Occupied Korea* is based on
his family's hardships in Korea.

People do not always write to tell an entertaining story. Sometimes people write to help understand themselves or the world around them. For Korean American writer Richard Kim, there was a lot to understand. "Originally, I had wanted to write about my grandfather's fate. . . . I tried to get inside his mind at the last moment of his life. . . . So I began to write—and then the novel took its own shape and course. I seemed to have tried to define myself in it."

The novel Kim refers to is *The Martyred,* which focuses on the Korean War of 1950-53. During that conflict, Kim's grandfather, who was a Christian missionary, was shot by Communist soldiers. Richard Kim was only 19 at the time of his grandfather's death, but already he had seen much cruelty and suffering.

Richard Kim, whose birth name was Kim Eun Kook (KIHM YOON KUK), was born in the northern part of Korea in 1932. Korea had fought with the Japanese both before and during World War II, as well as during the Korean War. "My family was always moving because my father—who had been jailed for anti-Japanese revolutionary activities—was a kind of political exile,"[1] Kim remembers.

In 1895 the Japanese and the Chinese had fought the Sino-Japanese War over who would control Korea. To the world's surprise, Japan defeated China, its much larger neighbor, and as a result, began to occupy Korea. Many Koreans fled the country, fearful about the future. Kim's family, however, decided to stay. Because he was seen as a rebel, Kim's father was beaten and imprisoned several times. Finally, the family moved north to

---

1. **exile** (EHKS-eyel) *n.* a person forced to leave his or her homeland

Manchuria, a region of China, which the Japanese had conquered but did not control so thoroughly.

In Manchuria, Kim attended kindergarten at a Christian missionary school. There he played with children from many different countries—China, England, Canada, the United States, and Korea. Before long, however, the missionaries were forced out of Manchuria. The Kims then returned to Korea to be with other family members during this time of struggle and oppression.[2]

Back in Korea, Kim went to a Japanese grade school. Here, children were not allowed to speak Korean. Even worse, the Korean children were assigned "new" Japanese names. Kim felt very angry about life under the Japanese. However, he later saw that Koreans could badly mistreat each other too. During World War II, he also learned that people of every nation are capable of cruelty toward one another. Years later, he would write about his feelings during the Japanese occupation as a way of understanding himself and of warning people everywhere about the horrors of war and political conflict.

Korea won its freedom at the end of World War II, but soon after this the Communists took control of what would become North Korea. The Kims fled to Seoul (SOHL), a city in the southern half of Korea. Richard was in his third week at the University of Seoul when the Korean War broke out, in June 1950. (See **Did You Know?** on page 20 for more information on North and South Korea.)

Dreadful things started happening fast. The Kims got word that the Communists had shot Richard's grandfather, who had stayed behind in the north. The Communists viewed missionary work as an act of rebellion. Then the Communists captured Seoul. They tried to force Richard and other men into their army. But Richard resisted, as his father and grandfather had done. He jumped from a second-story window and went into hiding. He refused to fight for the people who had killed his grandfather.

---

2. **oppression** (uh-PREHSH-uhn) *n.* harsh or cruel use of power

Three months later, United Nations (UN)[3] forces landed in South Korea. Richard immediately joined the army of South Korea. He served with honor, working with both Korean forces and U.S. forces from 1950 to 1954. Quick to learn languages, Kim used his knowledge of English, Chinese, Japanese, and Korean to help his side in the war.

Even during a war, good things can happen. One day Richard's army unit received some gifts from the United States. Because Kim knew English, it was his job to write thank-you notes for the "care" packages, as they were called. These notes led to a scholarship[4] from Middlebury College in Vermont. When the war was over, friends and relatives persuaded Richard to accept the scholarship.

As was so often true in his life, Kim faced challenges in the United States. "In my freshman year in college," the future writer admits, "I flunked all my composition courses." He then decided to concentrate on political science and history. Richard did well in these subjects, but because he failed two required courses—biology and chemistry—he did not get his degree. Not all was lost, though. Kim did meet Penelope Ann Groll at Middlebury, and they were married in 1960.

Later that year, Richard Kim received a fellowship from Johns Hopkins University. There he earned a Master of Arts degree in writing. Kim had finally discovered what he wanted to be. Penelope and Richard then moved to Iowa, where he enrolled in a writing workshop at the University of Iowa. In that creative writing program, Richard recalls, he learned the secret of good writing: "I used to be terrible, purple, verbose.[5] The most important thing I learned was cut, cut, cut."

While at Iowa working on a Master of Fine Arts degree,

---

3. **United Nations** (UN) an international organization of about 160 countries dedicated to maintaining world peace

4. **scholarship** (SKAHL-uhr-shihp) *n.* a gift of money or other aid to help a student pay for his or her education

5. **verbose** (vuhr-BOHS) *adj.* wordy

Richard began writing his first book, *The Martyred*. He finished the novel while he was at Harvard earning a third master's degree—this one in Far Eastern languages and literature. Richard Kim, the man who had once specialized in flunking classes, was now passing with flying colors—and doing so in some of the most demanding schools in the United States.

Kim, who was now used to success, found a publisher for his book. He was a little discouraged, though, when his editor, who was very impressed with Kim's work, warned him, "We may get some good reviews, Richard, but it won't sell." Fortunately, the editor was only half right. The book got great reviews, *and* it sold very well, too.

Richard E. Kim became a naturalized[6] citizen of the United States in 1964. Though still deeply attached to Korea, Kim felt that he had "never really developed an immutable[7] national identity from a political, social, and cultural point of view." The United States was his home.

However, in 1966, the time had come to return to Korea. "My parents and my friends in Korea had warned me that I would not be able to recognize the country and must be prepared for an emotional shock at seeing how different and changed everything was. They were quite wrong, for I found everything essentially unchanged," he notes sadly. From Kim's point of view, much about Korean life *should* have changed. To him, "The majority of Koreans are poor, miserable, suffering people, oppressed for centuries by governments and politicians, deceived by sweet-tongued political swindlers and jugglers." Kim left Korea in a dark mood.

Soon after his return to the United States, Richard Kim wrote an essay called "O My Korea!" in which he attacked the leaders of Korea for hypocrisy,[8] for creating the illusion[9] of freedom. It

6. **naturalized** (NACH-uhr-uhl-eyezd) *v.* to have become a citizen of a country one was not formerly a citizen of

7. **immutable** (ihm-MYOOT-uh-buhl) *adj.* never changing; permanent

8. **hypocrisy** (hih-PAHK-ruh-see) *n.* pretending to be something that one is not

9. **illusion** (ih-LOO-zhuhn) *n.* an imaginary or misleading appearance

is worse, he says, to live in a false democracy than to live in no democracy at all. What is his solution? "A genuine freedom will come only when those in power realize that their power is derived from those they govern . . . only when they are willing to hear even what they do not like."

His Korean heritage is the foundation of all of Kim's writing. In one of his most acclaimed books, *Lost Names: Scenes from a Boyhood in Japanese-Occupied Korea,* published in 1970, Richard Kim again reaches into the past for his story. *Lost Names* is about a Korean family's courage to survive terrible times. More than that, the book defines basic human rights and human dignity from a young person's point of view.

Kim feels Korea's hope for the future lies in the spirit of its people. He remembers a visit to Seoul. During this visit the Han River, along whose banks many poor people lived, looked as if it might flood. Kim writes: "The drenched have-nots in their cardboard huts along the Han River were thanking the merciful heaven laden with black rain clouds—Then the rain stopped, and once again the country was shimmering under the wondrously serene, clear blue sky."

> **Did You Know?** *Today, Korea is still divided into two sections: the Republic of Korea in the south and the Democratic People's Republic of Korea in the north. After World War II, China, the Soviet Union, Great Britain, and the United States tried to work together to help Korea recover from the Japanese occupation. However, they could not reach an agreement, so the country was divided along the 38th parallel of north latitude. The Soviet Union supported the Communist government in the north, and the United States supported the non-Communist government in the south. Soon, this split led to the Korean War (1950-53). Since 1954, there have been many international attempts to reunify Korea. Nevertheless, the Korean economy is growing, and the poor standard of living that Richard Kim describes is beginning to improve.*

AFTER YOU READ

EXPLORING YOUR RESPONSES

1. Richard Kim says he will never forget the anger he felt when Koreans were assigned Japanese names. How might you react if someone changed your name? Why?

2. Kim writes, in part, to tell the world about his heritage. If you were to write a novel, what might you write about and why?

3. Richard became a writer because he wanted to write about his grandfather's death and the destructiveness of war. What do you do when faced with a difficult situation?

4. The Kims returned to Korea to be with their family, even though they were in danger. What might you have done in this situation?

5. Even though Kim did not always do well in school, he kept on trying. How do you think his life might have been different if he had given up?

UNDERSTANDING WORDS IN CONTEXT

Read the following sentences from the biography. Think about what the underlined words mean. In your notebook, write what the word means as it is used in the sentence.

1. "My family was always moving because my father—who had been jailed for anti-Japanese revolutionary activities—was a kind of political exile."

2. The Kims then returned to Korea to be with other family members during this time of struggle and oppression.

3. These notes led to a scholarship from Middlebury College in Vermont.

4. "I used to be terrible, purple, verbose," he said. "The most important thing I learned was cut, cut, cut."

5. [In "O My Korea!"], he attacked the leaders of Korea for hypocrisy, for creating the <u>illusion</u> of freedom.

RECALLING DETAILS

1. Why did the Kims move to Manchuria?
2. Describe Richard's grade school in Korea.
3. What did Kim do while he was in the South Korean army?
4. Describe Kim's performance as a student in college and in graduate school.
5. Why did Kim begin to write?

UNDERSTANDING INFERENCES

In your notebook, write two or three sentences from the biography that support each of the following statements.

1. The people of Korea have experienced much hardship in the 20th century.
2. Richard Kim has adjusted to many different situations.
3. Writers can lead a very active life.
4. Richard Kim still loves his homeland.
5. Political conflict causes problems in many places, not just in Korea.

INTERPRETING WHAT YOU HAVE READ

1. Why do you think the Japanese gave the Koreans Japanese names?
2. Why do you think a "false democracy" might be worse than no democracy?
3. Why do you think Kim remains hopeful about Korea's future?
4. How did Richard feel about his Korean heritage when he was a child? When he was older?

5. When Kim returned to Korea in 1966, he was shocked to find things the same—not different. In what ways did he want things to be different?

ANALYZING QUOTATIONS

Read the quotation from the biography. Then answer the questions.

> Richard Kim once said of his relationship to Korea that he "never really developed an immutable national identity from a political, social, and cultural point of view."

1. What do you think Richard meant by this statement?
2. What are the pros and cons of having a strong national or cultural identity?
3. Do you think it is possible to value one's heritage without feeling a strong national identity? Explain.

THINKING CRITICALLY

1. Why do you think Richard Kim chose to be a writer?
2. Think about Richard's childhood in northern Korea. What events helped shape his view of himself?
3. What qualities did the Kim family have that helped them survive?
4. What do you think Richard hoped to find when he returned to Korea from the United States?
5. A critic said that in the novel *Lost Names,* Kim captured "the blazing resentment of the young." Do you think the young are more likely to have strong feelings—particularly about "how things should be"—than are older people? Explain.

DAVID HENRY HWANG

David Henry Hwang, Chinese American playwright, impressed audiences and critics with his play *M. Butterfly*. In this scene, B.D. Wong plays the role of a spy who poses as a Chinese actress.

Imagine that the last scene of a play called *M. Butterfly* has ended, and the lights of the theater have come on. People rise from their seats, page through their programs, look around to see how others are reacting to what they have just seen. As the audience files out of the theater, you hear people talking about the play's author, David Henry Hwang (WAHNG). They argue over what his plays are really about.

"He's too political," one man says. "All that heavy-handed stuff about racism[1] and imperialism[2] turns me off."

"I don't think those things are his main point," a woman disagrees. "Hwang's work is really about the difference between who we really are and who we think we should be."

"Yes," another woman chimes in. "It's also about sex stereotypes[3]—the 'ideal woman' that men want, and the clash when ideal meets reality."

It is hard to say which of these people is right. But one thing is sure: Chinese American playwright[4] David Henry Hwang has given people many things to talk about.

Hwang was born in Los Angeles in 1957. His father, Henry Hwang, was the head of a bank that lent money to Chinese immigrants. His mother, Dorothy, grew up in a rich and powerful Chinese merchant[5] family in the Philippines. David and his two

---

1. **racism** (RAY-sihz-uhm) *n.* the idea that one group of people is superior to another; racial prejudice
2. **imperialism** (ihm-PEER-ee-uh-lihz-uhm) *n.* a political system in which a powerful nation controls other nations or colonies
3. **stereotypes** (STEHR-ee-uh-teyeps) *n. pl.* rigid ideas about a person or group that allow for no individual differences
4. **playwright** (PLAY-reyet) *n.* a person who writes stories to be acted on a stage
5. **merchant** (MUHR-chuhnt) *adj.* having to do with buying and selling goods

sisters were raised in San Gabriel, a town near Los Angeles. Their home was much like those of their wealthy non-Chinese neighbors.

"I knew I was Chinese," Hwang later told an interviewer, "but growing up it never occurred to me that that had any particular implication[6] or that it should differentiate[7] me in any way. I thought it was a minor detail, like having red hair."

David's grandmother, though, did open a window for him on his Chinese heritage. She told what Hwang calls "talk-stories" about people in her family who lived long ago. Sometimes these stories revealed old fears and hinted at wounds that never healed. Once, for instance, she told the children not to get too close to the ocean. If they did, she said, they might be sold into slavery as one of their ancestors had been.

These stories meant so much to David that, when he was still quite young, he wrote a "sort of a novel" based on them. He made copies and gave them to his relatives. It would be some years, however, before he thought of himself as a writer again.

After graduating from high school in 1975, Hwang went to Stanford University in Palo Alto, California. There, he met other Asian American students who were exploring how they felt about their Asian and American heritages. In fact, Hwang began to spend most of his free time with other Asian Americans, including a stint[8] with an Asian American rock band called Bamboo.

As a result of these friendships, Hwang says, "I got more and more interested in responding to stereotypes by painting our own portraits." "Painting" full and accurate portraits of Asian Americans meant learning how to write well. So, David switched from studying law to studying writing and literature.

---

6. **implication** (ihm-plih-KAY-shuhn) *n.* something that is shown to have a connection with something else

7. **differentiate** (dihf-uhr-EHN-shee-ayt) *v.* to see differences between things

8. **stint** (STIHNT) *n.* a specified period of time doing something

Hwang now began going to plays at the Magic Theater in San Francisco. There he saw the work of Sam Shepard, a well-known playwright, and was inspired. Plays brought words and actions together. They showed people struggling with each other and learning who they really were. "I knew that I wanted to write things to create worlds, and then see the worlds right in front of me," Hwang says.

David Hwang's first attempt at writing a play was not successful. But, in 1978, he went to a summer workshop to work with Sam Shepard and other playwrights. There he wrote a play called *F.O.B.* These initials stand for "Fresh Off the Boat," the expression that Chinese Americans use jokingly to describe Chinese immigrants[9] who have just arrived in the United States.

F.O.B. explores the way Chinese Americans think about themselves. It also looks at U.S. society through an immigrant's eyes. David's teachers encouraged him to submit *F.O.B.* to the National Playwrights Conference, and remarkably, for a writer only 22 years old, it was accepted for production.

Meanwhile, Joseph Papp, at that time director of the New York Shakespeare Festival, was seeking new plays by Asian Americans. Papp liked the way *F.O.B.* blended U.S. and Asian acting techniques and contrasted Asian and U.S. cultures. He agreed to produce the play, which went on to win an Obie Award for best Off-Broadway play of the 1980–81 season.

In *Family Devotions*, which opened on October 18, 1981, Hwang reaches into his own past. The audience watches with amusement as a well-to-do Chinese American family scrambles for more money and status, or social position. Then, an uncle from China comes to visit. He forces his "live-for-today" relatives to look at "their connection to the past." Not everyone liked the play. Some critics said it was "a sort of Chinese 'I Love Lucy.'" There were those, though, who saw the play as "complex and fascinating." (See **Did You Know?** on page 29 for more

---

9. immigrants (IHM-uh-gruhnts) *n. pl.* people who come into a new country

information on traditional Chinese ideas about the meaning of life.)

With several plays produced in only a few years, Hwang was becoming a celebrity, a talked-about person in the theater world. He was viewed as a kind of spokesperson for Asian Americans. This bothered Hwang. Though flattered, he says, "it was no longer that I was [just a] playwright, but that I was an Asian American playwright, and my Asian Americanness became the quality which defined me to the public." Then came pressure from the other side. Some Asian American critics were saying that Hwang was continuing old stereotypes of the passive Asian.

Hwang now had a hard time writing. How could he please everyone—and still please himself as an artist? "My artistic motor had run out," he says. So, Hwang took a break to travel in Asia, Europe, and Canada. In 1985, he met a Chinese Canadian art student named Ophelia Chong, and they were married.

When he started writing again, Hwang tried something different. His next play, *Rich Relations,* opened on April 21, 1986. Again, the play is about a family's struggle with wealth. This time, however, he writes about white Americans, not Chinese Americans. The critics were unimpressed. They thought the play just repeated his earlier ideas. But Hwang also saw a problem with some of the critics: "There is in this country a misguided belief that women should write about women, blacks about blacks, the Chinese about Chinese. White males can write about anybody," he says. It was time for another break. Hwang wrote television and movie scripts for a while.

When he returned to the theater in 1988, it was with a bang. The title of his next play, *M. Butterfly,* comes from a famous opera called *Madama Butterfly,* in which a Japanese woman kills herself out of love for a British sailor. Many people see in the opera an example of stereotyping: the passive Asian woman and the conquering foreign "hero."

But *M. Butterfly* does more than question this stereotype. Hwang uses a real-life spy story to give the older story a twist. In Hwang's play, an official of the French government falls in love with a Chinese actress with the Beijing (BAY-JIHNG) Opera.

However, things aren't what they seem. The "actress" is a spy, and "she" is really a man in disguise. Characters changing roles, things looking one way but being another–these are themes that come up in many of Hwang's plays.

In part, the play deals with the attitudes of imperialists–Western powers that have seen Asia as a place they could take over. But the play also compares this imperialism with the way many men have treated women–as people they could take over. Finally, there is the mystery of how the French man could have become so close to this "woman" without accepting the truth. "Why are people so good at fooling themselves?" the play asks.

The critics disagreed about how successful the play is. Still, *M. Butterfly* won the Tony Award for the best Broadway play of 1988, as well as several other awards. It has earned more than $35 million–a statement about how much the public likes it.

David Hwang now deals with the problem many artists face after a popular triumph: "What do I do next? How do I top that?" His answer has been to write more plays that make people question their attitudes. As for the future, Hwang says he wants to write a very different kind of play, one that "deals with the small things that break your heart–I really want to do that next."

Did You Know? *The uncle in Hwang's play* Family Devotions *represents traditional Chinese attitudes that grow in part out of Daoism (DOW-ihzuhm), an ancient way of thinking and acting. According to Daoism, people should strive for a simpler, less self-centered life. They should also respect all living things and nature itself: nothing is more important than anything else. To some people raised in Western cultures, the idea that the "self" is not all-important seems strange and has contributed to the stereotype that Asians are "passive." Daoists, however, think that people should not try to "stand out." In the words of an ancient Daoist, "Perfect activity leaves no track behind it . . . like a jade worker whose tool leaves no mark."*

AFTER YOU READ

EXPLORING YOUR RESPONSES

1. When he was a child, David Henry Hwang thought that being Chinese was "a minor detail, like having red hair." Do you see your heritage as a "minor detail" or something more? Explain.

2. Some people think that *M. Butterfly* is about people who fool themselves. Why do you think that people sometimes talk themselves into something or "see what they want to see"?

3. Some people like Hwang's plays, and others find fault with them. When you disagree with a friend about a play, movie, or TV show, how do you resolve your disagreement?

4. Hwang uses the theater to make people question stereotypes. What are other ways of making people aware of stereotypes and the damage they can do?

5. In the play *F.O.B.*, Hwang shows that Chinese Americans can laugh at themselves. How do you and your friends use humor to understand something or to deal with a problem?

UNDERSTANDING WORDS IN CONTEXT

Read the following sentences from the biography. Think about what each underlined word means. In your notebook, write what the word means as it is used in the sentence.

1. "Yes," another woman chimes in. "It's also about sex stereotypes–the 'ideal woman' that men want, and the clash when ideal meets reality."

2. In fact, Hwang began to spend most of his free time with other Asian Americans, including a stint with an Asian American rock band called Bamboo.

3. "I knew I was Chinese . . . but growing up it never occurred to me that that had any particular implication or that it should differentiate me in any way."

4. These initials [F.O.B.] stand for "Fresh Off the Boat," the expression that Chinese Americans use jokingly to describe Chinese <u>immigrants</u> who have just arrived in the United States.

5. "I knew I was Chinese . . . but growing up it never occurred to me . . . that it should <u>differentiate</u> me in any way."

RECALLING DETAILS

1. How did Hwang decide to be a writer instead of a lawyer?
2. What was it about the theater that excited Hwang?
3. How did spending time with other Asian Americans in college change Hwang's views of his heritage?
4. Name one idea that appears in several of Hwang's plays.
5. How did the reaction of theater critics affect Hwang?

UNDERSTANDING INFERENCES

In your notebook, write two or three sentences from the biography that support each of the following inferences.

1. People have differing opinions about Hwang's plays.
2. What the critics said about Hwang's plays affected his writing.
3. Hwang's Asian American background affected his writing.
4. Hwang's plays make people think about themselves and society.
5. David's grandmother's "talk-stories" influenced his ideas about who he was.

INTERPRETING WHAT YOU HAVE READ

1. How do you think "painting our own portraits" might affect people's stereotyping of others?
2. Why do you think Hwang wrote plays instead of novels or poems?
3. After writing four plays and becoming successful, why did Hwang begin to have a hard time writing?

4. How do Hwang's plays reflect his Asian heritage?

5. Do you think Hwang is comfortable being a "celebrity"? Explain.

ANALYZING QUOTATIONS

Read the following quotation from the biography and answer the questions below.

> *"There is in this country a misguided belief that women should write about women, blacks about blacks, the Chinese about Chinese. White males can write about anybody."*

1. What does Hwang mean when he says, "White males can write about anybody"?

2. Do you think that writers should write only about people of their own gender and background? Explain.

3. If you were going to create a fictional character for a story or play, would you make that character very much like you or very different from you? Explain.

THINKING CRITICALLY

1. From what you have read in this biography about David Henry Hwang's plays, which one would you most like to see and why?

2. Do you think it would be possible for Hwang to write a play that would please everyone who saw it? Why or why not?

3. Why do you think David Henry Hwang's attitudes about his Chinese heritage changed while he was at Stanford University?

4. *M. Butterfly* suggests that people sometimes "wear disguises," or pretend to be what they aren't. When, if ever, do you think it's "right" for people to appear to be what they aren't?

5. When Hwang felt that his "artistic motor had run out," he took a break and traveled. What do you do when you feel as if your "motor" has run out?

VED MEHTA

Despite his impaired vision, Ved Mehta taught himself to ride
a bicycle. Although some of Mehta's writings are based on his
childhood in India, he writes about feelings and concerns that
are common to all people.

Amolak Ram Mehta (ahm-OH-lahk RAHM MAY-tuh) was recognized all over India as a leader in the fight against deadly diseases. But he could not help his son. When he was 3 years old, Ved Mehta (VEHD MAY-tuh) became seriously ill with meningitis (mehn-ihn-JEYET-ihs) and lost his sight.

Years later, Mehta recalled the sudden shift in the way he experienced the world: "I started living in a universe where it was not . . . the colors of the rainbow, a sunset or a full moon that mattered, but the feel of the sun against the skin, the slow drizzling sound of the spattering rain. . . . It was a universe where at first—but only at first—I made my way fumbling and faltering."[1]

Ved Metha was born in 1934 in Lahore, India. At the time, India was ruled by Great Britain, but was struggling to be free. When the country finally achieved independence after World War II, it was divided into two parts: India, which was intended to be for Hindus,[2] and Pakistan, which was intended to be for Muslims.[3] But fighting soon broke out between these two groups over religious and political differences. The Mehtas were Hindu, but Lahore had become a part of Muslim Pakistan. For no reason other than their religion, the Mehtas had their family house taken away. (See **Did You Know?** on page 38 for more information about Hindus and Muslims in India,)

During these difficult times, the government could not help visually impaired children very much. Ved spent some time,

---

1. **faltering** (FAWL-tuhr-ihng) *v.* moving in a hesitating, unsteady way
2. **Hindus** (HIHN-dooz) *n. pl.* followers of Hinduism, an ancient religion in India
3. **Muslims** (MUZ-luhms) *n. pl.* followers of Islam, the religion of Mohammed, which spread into India from the Arab world

though, at St. Dunstan's, a school for soldiers who had been blinded by injuries. Here Ved showed that he was bright and hard-working. He learned to read Braille, a kind of writing that uses patterns of raised dots to stand for letters and numbers. He also learned to type—a skill that would later help him succeed as a writer.

Ved Mehta refused to let his blindness stop him from getting where and what he wanted. Many of the soldiers at the school used guide wires[4] or sticks to find their way around. But Ved did not want to use a stick or to follow wires. He wanted more freedom.

At first, Ved often bumped into things and bruised himself, but he gradually improved his "facial vision." Some visually impaired people have developed this ability, which allows them to judge distances by the way sound bounces off them or by the way air puffs against their face. Later, Mehta would call this way of "seeing" things "sound shadows." Using this technique, Ved even taught himself to ride a bicycle.

By the time he was 15, however, Ved had learned everything that he could from Indian schools. His father tried to get him into a more advanced program abroad. Finally, after being rejected by 29 schools, Ved Mehta was accepted as a student by the Arkansas School for the Blind in Little Rock.

By the tenth grade, Ved was taking a heavy load of courses, including literature, world history, algebra, French, and music. He was also becoming interested in writing and journalism. He particularly liked biographies, which tell the true stories of people's lives.

Students at his school lived together in a big dormitory. During the summers, however, Ved could have a room of his own. He treasured his privacy and found it very difficult to return to the dormitory in the fall. However, the school had no

---

4. **guide wires** wires that visually impaired people can grasp and follow to a destination

rooms to spare. Then the principal, Mr. J. M. Woolly, allowed Ved to turn a tiny broom closet into his "office." Soon,
whenever some partially sighted students saw Ved, they would
exclaim, "It's Mr. Woolly's bat coming out of his black hole!"
Ved Mehta laughed with them. He had what he wanted—a place
of his own.

School life had its bitter surprises, though. Once a fellow
student told Ved that she didn't want to hear what a "darky" had
to say. Mehta noted in his diary: "I was enraged because Evelyn
dismissed my opinion on the grounds that my skin was darker
than hers. . . . She has this attitude, after all the education she has
received! More than ever I am determined to write a book one
day and discuss this attitude."

When Ved became interested in meeting young women, he
faced another big cultural difference between India and the
United States. In India, marriages were arranged by the couple's
parents. At the Arkansas school, however, boys and girls could
date whomever they wished. This seemed exciting, but also a bit
frightening.

Mehta's next challenge was college admission. When the day
came to take an important entrance test, Ved was dismayed[5] to
find that the Braille version he had requested was not available.
Even with the help of a reader, a person who assists the visually
impaired, he was unable to finish on time. Some of the math
diagrams were too complicated to explain. What was worse, the
testing people did not seem to care.

Finally, in 1952, Mehta was accepted at Pomona College in
Claremont, California. He was excited, but also lonely and
confused. Sometimes he felt that he "belonged to neither East
nor West, to neither India nor America."

Ved was also feeling the pressure from within to begin
writing. Part of that pressure came from a nagging doubt
regarding his own ability to write. Even when he was an

---

5. **dismayed** (dihs-MAYD) *adj.* suddenly disappointed or frightened

accomplished writer, Mehta noted that "however good you are, when you face the terror of a blank page, you find you don't know anything." The first time Ved seriously tried to write, he felt that terror and a resulting inability to put any words on paper.

"Just begin, begin anywhere," a voice inside said. Suddenly, he was back in his childhood, and he heard his father and mother having an argument. "My father came home one day and shouted at my mother, 'Your superstitions[6] will be the death of our family!' He had a fierce temper, and she had long since learned to bear it silently." The words then began to flow out swiftly. Later, these stories about his childhood became Mehta's first book, *Face to Face.*

After graduating from Pomona in 1956, he studied at Oxford University in England for three years, where he earned a degree in modern history. Originally, Mehta planned to teach college, but he ended up following his heart and becoming a writer. By 1961, he had joined the staff of the *New Yorker* magazine, for which he has since written regular articles on many subjects.

Some of Ved Mehta's writings are based on his own life—from early childhood experiences through his travels as an adult. Other writings introduce readers to the rich culture of India, to which he often returns. One book, *Portrait of India,* is a collection of essays first published in the *New Yorker.* This book shows his love for the diversity of his native land, but it also shows the pain he feels about the poverty, disease, and political fighting he still finds there.

Ved Mehta became a writer because "I wanted to see how I could exploit[7] my other senses," he once told an interviewer. "I wanted to explore my own life. . . . Partly I write because of blindness, because of the heightened sense of loneliness that many intelligent blind people feel."

---

6. **superstitions** (soo-per-STIHSH-uhns) *n. pl.* beliefs based on fear or a lack of knowledge
7. **exploit** (ehks-PLOIT) *v.* to use or take advantage of something

Writing has helped Ved Mehta make sense of his life—everything from the cruelty of prejudice to the mystery of love. "It's rather like being an archaeologist[8] of oneself, digging into oneself to see how one has become what one is now." But writing is about more than knowing yourself; it is about connecting with other people, too. As Mehta says, "All I'm trying to do is to tell a story not of one life, but of many lives—and through those stories, to try to say something that's universal."

Did You Know? *India gained its freedom from Great Britain in 1947. However, differences in beliefs divided Hindus and Muslims, the two largest religious groups in India. Muslims believed in one god and the equality of all Muslims. They also believed that Muslims should obey religious law strictly. Hindus, on the other hand, believed in many gods and based their society on the caste system, which divided people into rigid groups. Hindus also believed that people could interpret religious law in different ways.*

Great Britain thought that the only way to keep the two groups from starting a civil war would be to divide the country into two parts: India and Pakistan. In a panic to reach their assigned country, millions of people fled their homes. Hindus living in Pakistan fled to India, and Muslims living in India fled to Pakistan. In this great movement of people, rioting broke out and about 500,000 people were killed. Order was finally established, but religious unrest continues to trouble India and Pakistan.

---

8. **archaeologist** (ahr-kee-AHL-uh-jihst) *n.* a person who studies past civilizations

AFTER YOU READ

EXPLORING YOUR RESPONSES

1. After Ved Mehta lost his sight, he had to learn new ways of doing things. How do you think such a loss can help a person discover new interests?

2. Having privacy was very important to Ved Mehta. Do you enjoy privacy or do you prefer to be with other people most of the time? Explain.

3. Throughout his life, Mehta "refused to take *no* for an answer." Do you think that success depends on determination? Which other factors might also be involved?

4. Like many immigrants, Mehta had to adjust to the customs of a new country. How would you help a young person from a different culture make friends in your community?

5. Ved did not mind when students at the school in Arkansas teased him, calling him "Mr. Woolly's bat." How might you have reacted in this situation?

UNDERSTANDING WORDS IN CONTEXT

Read the following sentences from the biography. Think about what each underlined word means. In your notebook, write what the word means as it is used in the sentence.

1. "It was a universe where at first–but only at first–I made my way fumbling and faltering."

2. When the day came to take an important entrance test, Ved was dismayed to find that the Braille version he had requested was not available.

3. Many of the soldiers at the school used guide wires or sticks to find their way around. But Ved did not want to use a stick or to follow wires.

4. "I wanted to see how I could exploit my other senses. . .

because of the heightened sense of loneliness that many intelligent blind people feel."

5. "It's rather like being an <u>archaeologist</u> of oneself, digging into oneself to see how one has become what one is now."

RECALLING DETAILS

1. What was the political situation in India when Ved Mehta was growing up?

2. What are "sound shadows" and how did Ved use them?

3. What is the major difference between dating practices in India and the United States?

4. Why did Mehta come to the United States?

5. What are some of the things Mehta writes about?

UNDERSTANDING INFERENCES

In your notebook, write two or three sentences from the biography that support each of the following inferences.

1. Ved Mehta is someone who does not give up easily.

2. Mehta had to adjust to many new cultural expectations when he came to the United States.

3. Mehta cared about what other people thought of him.

4. Visually impaired people develop effective ways of "seeing."

5. India has experienced periods of religious unrest.

INTERPRETING WHAT YOU HAVE READ

1. Besides the nervousness everyone feels, why might Ved Mehta have felt anxious about dating?

2. Describe Mehta's relationship with his parents.

3. Some of the partially sighted students at Mehta's high school said, "It's Mr. Woolly's bat coming out of his black hole." Why might Mehta find this humorous?

4. How did Mehta's visual impairment affect his writing?

5. What frustrations did Mehta face because society did not always meet the needs of visually impaired people?

ANALYZING QUOTATIONS

Read the following quotation from the biography and answer the questions below.

> *"It's rather like being an archaeologist of oneself, digging into oneself to see how one has become what one is now, what kinds of decisions were made."*

1. An archaeologist learns about past civilizations and cultures by digging up artifacts—pottery, tools, weapons—that have been buried for centuries. How can a writer be thought of as an archaeologist?

2. How might "digging" up memories help a person start to write?

3. Do you prefer to write about your life or about subjects you have to research? Why?

THINKING CRITICALLY

1. What does Ved's refusal to use sticks and guide wires tell you about his attitude toward his disability?

2. Ved Mehta has interviewed many people during his writing career. If you could interview him, what two questions would you ask? Explain.

3. Mehta was puzzled by the prejudice he encountered in the United States. Why do you think it surprised him?

4. Which of Ved Mehta's qualities do you admire most? How might you develop that quality further in yourself?

5. How do you think Mehta's life might have been different if he had not lost his sight?

YOSHIKO UCHIDA

Yoshiko Uchida (left), Japanese American writer, is shown here at age 10 with her mother, father, grandmother, and older sister Keiko (right). Proud of her cultural heritage, Uchida wrote about Japanese American traditions, hopes, and values.

Yoshiko Uchida (yoh-SHEE-koh oo-CHEE-dah) spent the afternoon of December 7, 1941, studying for final exams. She was a senior at the University of California at Berkeley, and a bright future was just within reach. Then, everything changed. She returned to her home of 15 years to find her world torn apart.

Yoshiko's father was not there. Her mother, Iku (EE-koo), was serving tea to an FBI[1] agent, who was explaining that Dwight Takashi (tah-KAH-shee) Uchida was being held for questioning. Mr. Uchida had not been accused of any wrongdoing, the agent assured the family. He was being questioned only because he had been born in Japan.

Earlier that day, the Uchidas had listened with disbelief to the news that Japanese planes had bombed U.S. bases in Pearl Harbor, Hawaii. They did not know then, however, that this event signaled the start of war between the United States and Japan. The family learned later that most Japanese American business and community leaders in California, Dwight Uchida among them, were arrested soon after the bombing.

The months and years that followed seemed like a nightmare. The Uchidas had thought of themselves as full-fledged[2] members of U.S. society. Mr. and Mrs. Uchida had lived in the United States for many years, although the law would not let them become citizens. They were Issei (EE-SAY), or Japanese who had moved permanently to the United States—Dwight in 1906 and Iku in 1916. "Their loyalty and devotion to their adopted country was vigorous and strong," Yoshiko Uchida wrote later of her parents.

---

1. **FBI** (Federal Bureau of Investigation) a government agency that investigates crimes against the United States
2. **full-fledged** (FOOL FLEHJD) *adj.* complete; completely developed

In addition, the Uchida children were both born in the United States—Yoshiko in 1921, and her older sister, Keiko (KAY-koh), four years earlier. They were Nisei (NEE-SAY), or Japanese Americans who were born in the United States.

Mr. Uchida was imprisoned in Montana for five months, and the rest of the family, like most of the Japanese Americans who lived on the West Coast at that time, was arrested and sent to an internment camp. (See **Did You Know?** on page 47 for more information on internment camps.) They were arrested, as Yoshiko Uchida wrote later, "simply because we looked like the enemy." In addition to losing their homes, people also lost their names. The Uchidas became Family #13453.

A few brave Japanese Americans resisted this unfair treatment. Most, however, were too shocked and frightened to protest. "The world then was totally different from the one we know today," Uchida wrote. "In 1942 the voice of Martin Luther King had not yet been heard and ethnic pride was yet unborn. There was no awareness in the land of civil rights. . . . Most Americans, supporting their country in a war they considered just . . . might well have considered it treasonous[3] had we tried to resist or protest."

How could Yoshiko leave her wonderful house, with its garden full of fruit trees and flowers? In a book Uchida wrote years later about this difficult time, a character says, "How can I pack our whole life into boxes and cartons in just ten days?"

In May 1942, the entire Uchida family was sent to the Tanforan Race Track in San Bruno, California. There they lived for four months, surrounded by barbed wire, with about 8,000 other Japanese Americans. Each family lived in a whitewashed horse stall. There was little room, and less privacy.

Yoshiko was not allowed to attend graduation ceremonies at Berkeley. Instead, her diploma[4] arrived in the mail. But Yoshiko

---

3. **treasonous** (TREE-zuh-nuhs) *adj.* involving acts that are intended to overthrow the government of a person's own country

4. **diploma** (dih-PLOH-muh) *n.* a document saying that someone has graduated from a school or college

Uchida had little time to feel bad; she was busy teaching second-grade children at the camp.

In September 1942, the Uchidas were sent to another camp, in Topaz, Utah. This location—a bare, dusty lake bed—was no improvement on the race track. "With each step we sank two or three inches deep, sending up swirls of dust that crept into our eyes and mouths, noses and lungs," Yoshiko remembers. "Much of our energy simply went into keeping our room dusted, swept, and mopped." Life was becoming intolerable.

A group called the Student Relocation Committee helped Yoshiko win a fellowship[5] to study at Smith College in Massachusetts. The committee also found work for Yoshiko's sister Keiko in a nursery school near Smith. The sisters left Topaz in May 1943. Their parents were released later that year and went to live in Salt Lake City.

Yoshiko Uchida got a master's degree in education from Smith in 1944. She then taught school for a year, but found that teaching left her no time for writing—her secret passion. So, Uchida headed for New York City, where Keiko was a teacher, and took a job as a secretary. Now she had time to write at night.

Most of the stories Uchida wrote for adults were rejected, so she began writing stories for children. Uchida's first children's book, *The Dancing Kettle,* based on Japanese folktales she had heard while growing up, was published in 1949. A new life was beginning.

In 1952, Uchida won a grant[6] from the Ford Foundation in recognition of her folktale book. With the grant money, Yoshiko went to study in Japan for two years. She found that she "loved everything about the country" and became more aware of her Japanese heritage.

---

5. **fellowship** (FEHL-oh-shihp) *n.* a gift of money that pays for a graduate student's or scholar's studies

6. **grant** (GRANT) *n.* a gift of money to be used to work on a project

Yoshiko had always been proud of being Japanese American. Still, while growing up, she had tried hard to be just like her non-Japanese classmates, as most Nisei of her time did. Try though she might, Yoshiko could not become one of "them." Even little things hurt. Once, for instance, a woman told her, "You speak English so beautifully," not realizing that Yoshiko had been born in the United States. She had been hurt, too, when classmates did not invite her to their parties because she was "different." After her trip to Japan, however, Uchida "came home . . . with new respect and admiration for the culture that had made my parents what they were."

By 1955, Yoshiko Uchida was living again in Berkeley and writing fulltime. Most of her books, from this point on, were stories for children, and many have won awards. Some are collections of folktales, and others are tales about children living in Japan. Uchida's work introduces children to the customs and ancient values of Japan. They also speak about the problems and feelings children anywhere might have. "With so much in all of us that is alike, it is a pity people . . . have continued to find so much in each other that is different and strange," Uchida wrote. She knew very well how being thought "strange" can affect a person.

In 1966, Yoshiko Uchida decided to write a book for her parents and the other Issei "who had endured so much and been so strong." It would be 1971, however, before Uchida had sorted through all her feelings and found the words to express them. *Journey to Topaz* is fiction,[7] but the story is based on the Uchida family's experiences at the camp in Topaz. Later, she wrote a sequel[8] called *Journey Home.* Uchida says she wrote this book because so many young readers wrote to ask her what had happened to the Sakane (suh-KAH-neh) family in *Journey to Topaz.*

---

7. **fiction** (FIHK-shuhn) *n.* a story that is invented or made up rather than true life

8. **sequel** (SEE-kwuhl) *n.* a story that continues an earlier story

Uchida, who died in 1992, often spoke to groups of children about these books. "I always ask the children why they think I wrote *Journey to Topaz* and *Journey Home.* . . . 'To tell about the camps?' they ask. 'To tell how you felt? To tell what happened to the Japanese people?' 'Yes,' I answer, but I continue . . . until finally one of them will say, 'You wrote those books so it won't ever happen again.'"

Yoshiko Uchida wrote for many reasons. One was personal. She wanted to "preserve the magic as well as the joy and sadness of certain moments in my life." Uchida also wanted to teach Japanese American children about their rich heritage. "I feel it's so important for Japanese American–and all Asian American–children to be aware of their history and culture, and to understand some of the traditions, hopes, and values of the early immigrants," she said.

There was a third reason. "I write for *all* children. . . . I try to stress the positive aspects of life that I want children to value and cherish. I hope they can be caring human beings who don't think in terms of labels–foreigners or Asians or whatever–but think of people as human beings. If that comes across, then I've accomplished my purpose."

Did You Know? *In 1942, the U.S. government became fearful that some Japanese Americans might be spies or might try to help Japan in some way. As a result, the government interned, or confined, about 120,000 Japanese Americans living on the West Coast in special camps. These camps were like military bases. They had one large mess hall and group bathrooms. Families had very little privacy. Meanwhile, 17,000 patriotic Japanese Americans were fighting in Europe against the Nazis.*

In 1983, a government commission concluded that fear and prejudice, not national security, were behind the internment. Uchida wrote that by imprisoning Japanese

Americans, "our leaders betrayed not only the Japanese Americans, but all Americans. . . . By denying the Constitution, they damaged the very essence of our democratic beliefs."

AFTER YOU READ

EXPLORING YOUR RESPONSES

1. Although her early stories were rejected, Uchida kept writing. Do you think it is always a good idea to keep doing something even when you do not succeed at first?

2. Uchida's trip to Japan made her more aware of her heritage. How can traveling to a new place change a person's attitudes?

3. Uchida loved talking with children. What do you think adults can learn from children?

4. Yoshiko always tried to emphasize the similarities—not the differences—among groups of people. Do you think there are more similarities than differences? Explain.

UNDERSTANDING WORDS IN CONTEXT

Read the following sentences from the biography. Think about what each underlined word means. In your notebook, write what the word means as it is used in the sentence.

1. In 1952, Uchida won a grant from the Ford Foundation in recognition of her folktale book.

2. "Most Americans, supporting their country in a war they considered just . . . might well have considered it treasonous had we tried to resist or protest."

3. *Journey to Topaz* is fiction, but the story is based on the Uchida family's experiences at the camp in Topaz.

4. Later she wrote a sequel [to *Journey to Topaz*] called *Journey Home* because so many young readers wrote to ask her what had happened to the Sakane family in *Journey to Topaz*.

5. The Uchidas had thought of themselves as full-fledged members of U.S. society. Mr. and Mrs. Uchida had lived in the United States for many years.

RECALLING DETAILS

1. Why was the Uchida family sent to an internment camp?

2. Describe the conditions at the two internment camps in which the Uchidas lived.

3. What did Yoshiko Uchida learn while in Japan?

4. How have children shown their appreciation for Uchida's books?

5. What are *Journey to Topaz* and *Journey Home* about?

UNDERSTANDING INFERENCES

In your notebook, write two or three sentences from the biography that support each of the following inferences.

1. Japanese Americans were treated unfairly during World War II.

2. Yoshiko Uchida has made being "different" an advantage.

3. At the time of the Uchidas' internment, people often did not protest unfair treatment.

4. Uchida hoped her writing might help people understand one another.

5. The way people look can affect the way they are treated.

INTERPRETING WHAT YOU HAVE READ

1. A character in one of Uchida's books cries, "How can I pack our whole life into boxes and cartons in just ten days?" What feelings do these words express about being uprooted?

2. While growing up, Yoshiko tried hard to be like her non-Japanese classmates. Why and when do you think she stopped behaving in this way?

3. How can being thought "strange" affect a person?

4. How do Yoshiko's writings reflect her Japanese heritage?

5. Why do you think Yoshiko Uchida decided to teach children while in the internment camp?

ANALYZING QUOTATIONS

Read the following quotation from the biography and answer the questions below.

> *When talking about the children for whom she writes, Yoshiko said, "I hope they can be caring human beings who don't think in terms of labels—foreigners or Asians or whatever—but think of people as human beings."*

1. What does it mean to think of others "in terms of labels"?

2. Labels focus on people's differences rather than their similarities. What would the world be like without labels?

3. Why do you think people use labels? Do you think all labels are harmful or just some? Explain.

THINKING CRITICALLY

1. While the Japanese Americans were living at Tanforan they set up schools and churches. Why do you think they did this?

2. What do you think might have happened if Japanese Americans had refused to go to the internment camps?

3. Think about what you learned about life in the United States in 1942. What can you see that is different from life today, and what is the same?

4. How do you think Uchida's life might have been different if there had been no internment camps?

5. The United States has been called a "melting pot." Do you think Uchida would consider people of different cultural backgrounds "melting" together a good thing? Explain.

CULTURAL CONNECTIONS

Thinking About What People Do

1. Choose one writer in the unit and make notes on some of that person's early experiences. Then write two paragraphs in your notebook in which you imagine how that person's life might have been different without those experiences.

2. Most successful writers were influenced by other writers. Imagine you are one of the writers in this unit and write a "thank-you" note to someone who has influenced you. Mention several ways in which this person has helped your work.

3. With a partner, choose one writer in this unit and recall what you have learned about the way he or she became successful. Make up a dialogue with your partner in which one of you pretends to be the writer and the other pretends to be a writing student. Have the "writer" advise the "writing student" on how to become successful. Present your dialogue to the class.

Thinking About Culture

1. Most of the writers discussed in this unit had to endure many hardships. Choose two writers and explain, using examples, how one writer's hardships were similar to those of another writer.

2. Name several situations in which the writers in this unit felt that they did not fit into U.S. culture. What did they do either to fit in better or to change their ideas of what fitting in means?

3. How do you think a person's cultural heritage affects the way he or she lives and works? Give examples from people's lives you know about or from the biographies in this unit.

Building Research Skills

Work with a partner to complete the following activity.

Choose the person discussed in this unit whose work or life story interests you. Make a list of questions that were not answered in this biography. Your questions might include:

> **Hint:** The Bibliography at the back of this book lists articles and books to help you begin your research.

☆ What kind of education does the writer have?

☆ Did the writer attend school in the United States or in another country?

☆ Who helped the writer develop his or her skills?

☆ Did the writer's family and friends support his or her career choice? If so, how did they show this support?

> **Hint:** Think about places in the biographies where you thought, "Why did Amy Tan write speeches for other people instead of writing her own work?" or "How did Ved Mehta learn to get around in unfamiliar cities?"

☆ How does the writer find ideas for his or her writing?

☆ What styles does the writer use?

☆ What other writers have influenced his or her work?

Next, go to the library to look for information that will answer your questions.

Present your findings to the class in an oral report. You might include photographs of the writer in your presentation or display his or her books.

Extending Your Studies

GEOGRAPHY **Your task:** *To chart geographical locations using longitude and latitude.* As you learned in Richard Kim's biography, Korea was divided into two sections—North Korea and South Korea—after World War II. The geographical division between North Korea and South Korea is the 38th parallel. What does this mean?

If you look at a globe, you will see horizontal and vertical lines circling the earth. The vertical lines are called *lines of longitude,* or *meridians.* The horizontal lines are called *lines of latitude,* or *parallels.* The horizontal line that circles the middle of the earth is called the *equator.* Now find the 30th and 45th parallels of north latitude. (Lines above the equator are referred to as *north.*) Next, find North Korea and South Korea. As you can see, the division falls on the 38th parallel.

Work with a small group to find North Korea and South Korea on a globe. Then answer these questions:

☆ Are North Korea and South Korea north or south of the equator?

☆ Between what lines of latitude and longitude are North Korea and South Korea located?

As a group, choose one country in Asia for further study. Determine between which lines of longitude and latitude the country is located, then determine the location of the country's capital and two other major cities.

Play Where in the World Am I? with the class by reading aloud the longitude and latitude lines you have worked out. Have the rest of the class guess which country and cities match the longitudes and latitudes you present.

LANGUAGE ARTS **Your task:** *To write a book review.* You learned in Yoshiko Uchida's biography that she wrote many books for young adults, including *Journey to Topaz, Journey Home, In-Between Miya, Hisako's Mysteries,* and *The Sea of Gold and Other Tales from Japan.* Read one of Uchida's works and write a review to share with your classmates. As you write your book review, keep in mind the following:

Do	Don't
☆ write a summary	☆ tell every detail
☆ give your own opinion	☆ give away the ending

Present your review to the class, then assemble all of the reviews into a class Critic's Corner.

MATH **Your task:** *To develop a scale that identifies authors' royalties on book sales.* The amount of money an author earns often depends on how many copies of the book are sold. The author then earns *royalties,* or a percentage of the selling price, on books that are sold.

You learned in Amy Tan's biography that she received an *advance* to write her first book. An advance is money that an author is paid before a book is completed. As the book sells, the advance is subtracted from the royalties the author earns. Once the advance is "paid off," the author receives royalty payments.

Consider this example: An author is given a $10,000 advance against future royalties of 10 percent. When the book is completed, it sells for $15.00. This means that the author receives $1.50 for every book sold. How many books have to be sold for the author to "pay back" the advance? (*Hint:* Divide 10,000 by 1.50.) How many books have to be sold for the author to earn $50,000? Work with a partner to develop a situation in which an author with a 10-percent royalty becomes a millionaire.

WRITING WORKSHOP

When you write the story of your own life, it is called an **autobiography**. In many ways, writing about yourself may not seem difficult. After all, who knows you better than you know yourself? Even so, autobiographical writing can be challenging.

In this lesson, you will write an **autobiographical essay** about one event in your life. This event should reveal something about your personality or character. In your essay, you will share your thoughts with your classmates. Another student will assist you in editing your work. Having a classmate's point of view will help you ensure that your work makes sense and is enjoyable to read.

PREWRITING

Before you start to write, think about your topic, organize your thoughts, and take notes. This first step in the writing process is called *prewriting*. You can use several different prewriting strategies to get started. Here are two suggestions:

Listing: On a blank sheet of paper, make three columns. Label the columns *Events, People,* and *Places.* Use the following chart as a guide:

Events	People	Places

Work quickly to fill in these columns, noting any memories that come to you. For example, you might list changes in your life, such as a move or a new family member. The things you list can be big events or little ones. Just get the ideas down, filling each column if you can. When your page is filled, you will have many ideas to choose from to write your essay.

Asking questions: Explore your topic further by asking yourself questions about some of the events of your life. For example, choose one of the events or ideas from your list. Write it at the top of another blank sheet of paper. Then think of as many questions as you can that relate to that idea. Your questions should help you analyze the event. Here are some questions to help you begin:

☆ How old was I?

☆ What happened?

☆ Who else was involved?

☆ What did I think of the event at the time?

☆ What do I think of it now?

☆ Why was the event important?

☆ What did the event mean to me?

☆ What does the event or the way I dealt with it say about me?

Review your lists of ideas and questions. Write down some answers to your questions and any additional details that will help your reader form a clear picture of you. Your answers do not have to be complete sentences. Be sure to include ideas and details that will help your reader see the real you.

Organizing: Next, put your ideas in a clear and understandable order. You will probably write about your event *chronologically*, that is, in the sequence in which the events happened. Arrange your notes in the order in which you will use them.

DRAFTING

Now you can begin writing or **drafting** your autobiographical essay. You may want to keep the following strategies in mind as you write:

Use colorful language: Include vivid details that will appeal to your reader's senses: sight, hearing, smell, touch, and taste. Try to catch your reader by surprise at the beginning and hold that interest. Be honest about yourself and the events you are describing.

Use dialogue: Using the actual words of people adds life and variety to your writing. Choose words that help reveal your personality and that of others if you can.

Tell an exciting story: Do not worry about making your draft perfect. You will check for word usage and spelling errors later.

REVISING

Put your essay aside for a day or two. Then, with the help of another student who will act as your editor, evaluate and **revise** your work. See the directions for writers and student editors below.

Directions for Writers: Read your work aloud. Listen to how it flows. Ask yourself the following questions:

☆ Is my writing clear?

☆ Are the ideas in order?

☆ Do the sentences make sense?

☆ Did I include interesting details?

☆ Have I drawn a picture of my event so my readers can see it in their minds?

☆ Have I shown my readers why this event was important to me?

Make notes for your next draft or revise your work before you give it to a student editor. Then ask the student editor to read your work. Listen carefully to his or her suggestions. If they seem helpful, use them to improve your writing when you revise your work.

Directions for Student Editors: Read the work carefully and respectfully, remembering that your purpose is to help the writer do his or her best work. Keep in mind that an editor should always make positive, helpful comments that point to specific parts of the essay. After you read the work, use the following questions to help you direct your comments:

☆ What did I like most about the essay?

☆ What would I like to know more about?

☆ Can I see the scene or event in my mind?

☆ Do I understand what the event means to the writer?

PROOFREADING

When you are satisfied that your work says what you want it to say, check it carefully for errors in spelling, punctuation, capitalization, and grammar. Then make a neat, final copy of your autobiographical essay.

PUBLISHING

After you revise your autobiographical essay, you are ready to publish it. Prepare a title page that states the title of your work and includes your name as the author. Then create a cover with illustrations or graphics that help portray the real you. Display your essay as part of a class Who's Who.

UNIT 2

ASIAN AMERICANS IN FINE ARTS AND COMMUNICATION

In this unit, you will read about five Asian Americans who made great strides in the arts. What do these people have in common? What makes each one special? As you read the unit, think about each person's cultural background and how it helped shape that person's life. Also think about what each of these quotes from the subjects says about his or her life and work.

The Japanese American sculptor, **Isamu Noguchi**, observed, "I am the fusion of two worlds, the East and West. . . . Yet I hope I reflect more than both."

Maya Lin is a Chinese American who feels strongly about being an architect, in part because she is a woman. She says, "I'm determined to prove that women can get things built."

An illustrator of children's books, **José Aruego**, who was born in the Philippines, feels humor is important in his work. He says, "[My] ideas must have humor. . . . If they are serious, I cannot get my juices working."

Connie Chung, the Chinese American journalist and newscaster, says about her trip to China in 1987, "I think it was meaningful to the viewers, because it was *my* family. My life has been much more defined by my roots since that experience."

The Chinese American architect, **I. M. Pei**, remarks, "You would think that, blessed with this kind of beauty, the architecture would come easy. But it doesn't. . . . When you are confronted with nature, you just don't try to compete with it. You try to join with it."

After reading the biographies, refer again to the quotes above. Decide if they are good summarizing statements about each person. If you would choose a different quote, which would you choose?

ISAMU NOGUCHI

Isamu Noguchi, Japanese American sculptor, stands beside one of his creations. Noguchi's works express his desire to fuse his Japanese and American heritages.

You are walking in a garden, and something catches your eye. It is a stone sculpture[1] that looks like four giant loaves of bread huddled together. You read the title of the piece, *The Illusion[2] of the Fifth Stone.* Puzzled, you count the stones again. Yes, there are only four, but there *is* a space where a fifth stone would fit. Aha! Suddenly you realize that the artist had *wanted* you to think about that fifth stone. The thought is part of this artistic creation.

The Illusion of the Fifth Stone is only one example of how Japanese American sculptor Isamu Noguchi (ih-SAHM-oo nuh-GOOT-chee) helped people see art in new ways. In his long career, Noguchi showed that sculpture is more than silent statues or cold, twisted shapes of steel. He helped people see that sculpture can sing and dance and play in addition to encouraging thought.

Many of Noguchi's most important designs are not found in museums. They are in places where people can be part of them. Some are stage sets[3] for actors and dancers. Others are gardens that invite people to sit quietly and enjoy nature's beauty. Still others are playgrounds for family gatherings. How did Noguchi come to create works that are exciting to both a trained art critic and a child? Perhaps his desire and ability to bring together different worlds came, in part, from his own life story. In his life, Noguchi often felt the pull of different influences.

Isamu Noguchi's life had a rocky start. He was born in Los Angeles, California, in 1904. His father, Yone (YOH-nay)

---

1. **sculpture** (SKULP-cher) *n.* the art of carving, welding, or molding wood, stone, metal, or other materials into statues or forms

2. **illusion** (ih-LOO-zhuhn) *n.* something that is unreal, deceiving, or not really there

3. **sets** (SEHTS) *n. pl.* scenery and objects used to provide a background for a stage play or dance performance

Noguchi, was a poet who had come to the United States from Japan. Leonie (lee-OH-nee) Gilmour, Isamu's mother, was born in the United States. A writer and teacher, she was of Irish and Native American descent.

The couple stayed together only a short time. Before Isamu was 2 years old, his father returned to Japan. Two years later, Leonie and Isamu followed, hoping for a reunion. Leonie soon discovered, however, that Yone had married a Japanese woman and was no longer interested in his son.

Leonie and Isamu stayed in Japan until the boy was 13 years old. Then Leonie sent Isamu alone to a school in the United States. Noguchi later described his feeling at this time of being "neither Japanese nor American—that has always been a trouble. In many ways, I'm like a soldier in a campaign[4] in the desert—far off, but always with the idea that there's some place that I'm going back to someday."

As a teenager, Isamu Noguchi became interested in sculpture. His first sculpture teacher, however, told him that he had no talent. Noguchi began to study to be a medical doctor instead. Then another sculptor saw young Noguchi's talent. He arranged a show of Noguchi's work in New York City. Soon after, Noguchi quit medical school to be a sculptor full time.

By the age of 21, Noguchi was well known in the New York art world. He was not completely happy with his career, however. Then, in 1926, Noguchi saw an exhibit of Romanian sculptor Constantin Brancusi's (BRAHN-koosh) work that stunned him. Unlike most sculptors of the time, Brancusi did not make sculptures that copied all the details of real persons or things. Rather, he used shapes to suggest ideas or feelings. For example, his sculpture *Bird in Space* used simple, curving pieces of metal to capture the feeling of a bird in flight rather than including a bird in the work.

Fascinated by what he had seen and eager to use these new ideas, Noguchi applied for and received a Guggenheim (GOO-

---

4. **campaign** (kam-PAYN) *n.* a series of connected battles in a war

guhn-heyem) Fellowship. This gift of money allowed him to study in Paris, France, where Brancusi lived. Soon after arriving, Noguchi visited Brancusi's studio.[5] The famed sculptor said that he did not accept students. Noguchi then asked if he could simply cut stone. Brancusi agreed. As he worked, Noguchi became fascinated with stone—its shape, feel, and weight. Later in his career, he described stone as "a direct link to the heart of matter. . . . When I tap it, I get the echo of that which we are."

In the 1930s, just as Brancusi and Noguchi were creating a new kind of modern sculpture, well-known U.S. dancer Martha Graham was inventing a kind of dancing that expressed feelings in new ways. Many of her dances retold stories from long ago. She asked Noguchi, who was always interested in extending his art to new areas, to make stage sets during the 1930s that helped Graham and her dancers to capture the mood of these unusual stories.

For example, one of Graham's dance pieces is called *Cave of the Heart*. This dance retells an ancient Greek story about Jason and Medea (mih-DEE-uh*). Medea loves Jason, but Jason has fallen in love with a princess. Medea becomes so jealous and angry that she kills the princess. Part of Noguchi's stage set for the dance is a spiky, cagelike brass sculpture. After the murder, the dancer playing Medea puts this sculpture over her body to wear it like a harness. In this way, the sculpture is transformed from a stage set to a costume. As the dancer moves around the stage, the brass rays of the sculpture glitter and quiver.

It was also in the 1930s that Noguchi began to think about how people might not only see and touch sculpture, but actually play on and with it. One sculpture playground he designed was called *Play Mountain*. Imagine now that you are a young child who visits *Play Mountain*. You find the ground tilted up at all sorts of angles. You slide down the side of a pyramid. Later, you and your friends play tag or hide and seek, darting in and out of the openings underneath the pyramid. In winter, you can race

---

5. studio (STOO-dee-oh) *n.* the working place of a painter, sculptor, or photographer

your sled down a twisting, turning spiral.[6] There is a pool of water for wading in summer. On a sunny day, a band may be playing by the side of the playground.

Noguchi could not get the New York Parks Commission to agree to build *Play Mountain*. But much later, in 1976, he was able to build a new playground in Atlanta, Georgia, that included a giant "sculpture" that was also a slide.

As much as Noguchi liked to experiment with new ways to get his artistic messages across, he also chose to explore the artistic traditions of his Japanese heritage. (See **Did You Know?** on page 67 for more information on Noguchi's influence on modern Japanese art.) For example, Noguchi became quite fond of working with clay after studying the Japanese art of pottery-making. Pottery is made of clay that is hardened by being baked in a special oven. Noguchi saw clay as "a natural medium[7] to work with there [in Japan]. I associate it with the closeness of earth and wood which is for me Japan." In the 1940s, Noguchi also began to experiment with the traditional Japanese garden as an art form. In such a garden, every object is carefully chosen both for its physical beauty and its symbolic[8] meaning. Even the space between objects is not seen as mere emptiness. The space is a "presence" with its own shape and importance. *The Illusion of the Fifth Stone* and some other Noguchi sculptures that were meant to be placed in gardens use this Japanese idea of space.

Noguchi began to make "sculpture gardens." These were places, usually outdoors, where people walked in, around, over, and among carefully placed sculptures. For example, Noguchi designed a pair of bridges for the Park of Peace in Hiroshima, Japan. This city had been largely destroyed by an atomic bomb during World War II. Noguchi's design for the bridges brings together the ideas

6. **spiral** (SPEYE-ruhl) *n.* a design that curves around and around a central point while getting larger or smaller

7. **medium** (MEE-dee-uhm) *n.* a material or a way of working used by an artist

8. **symbolic** (sihm-BAHL-ihk) *adj.* representing or suggesting something else

of life and death. One bridge ends in a circle that balances on it like a rising, life-giving sun. The other bridge is shaped like one of the curved boats that ancient Egyptians used to send the dead on their journey to the next world. Walking over these bridges makes people think of the journey between life and death.

Noguchi did not want his great success to make him lazy. He did not want to do the same kind of work over and over, no matter how well people liked it. "I think success is a very dangerous thing," he said, "because you become immediately less free than when you were less successful. So, I'm still a struggling artist–at least in my own eyes." He used the feeling of struggling to make himself go on trying new things.

Noguchi never retired. At the age of 84, he traveled to Sapporo, Japan, to design a park. He also went to Italy to choose stone for new sculptures. But in this same year, 1988, he died.

When Isamu Noguchi died, people tried to find words to describe this man and his achievements. Perhaps the best words are Noguchi's own. In a 1968 interview he said, "I am the fusion[9] of two worlds, the East and West. . . . Yet I hope I reflect more than both."

> **Did You Know?** *Isamu Noguchi was truly a bridge between the East and the West, the old and the new. As you have read, he was influenced by ancient Japanese pottery. Noguchi, in turn, influenced the younger generation of Japanese sculptors. Beginning in 1949, Noguchi began to visit Japan frequently. The Japanese sculptors followed traditional artistic styles that were hundreds of years old. Modern and Western-style art was not generally accepted at this time. Yet, Noguchi's work interested the younger sculptors. They adapted his ideas in their own work. Although traditional art was still the norm in Japan, beginning in the 1950s, because of Noguchi's influence, a modern sculpture style began to appear in Japan.*

---

9. fusion (FYOO-zhun) *n.* a union of two things

AFTER YOU READ

EXPLORING YOUR RESPONSES

1. Look at the photo of Noguchi's work on page 62. Describe what you see and what it makes you think about.

2. Early in Noguchi's career, people showed interest in his talent as a sculptor. How has someone helped you develop a talent? Explain.

3. As an artist, Noguchi often tried new ways of expressing himself. In your experience, what are the pros and cons of trying something new?

4. Noguchi associated clay, earth, and wood with Japan. What natural elements do you associate with the place you live?

5. Noguchi wanted to make art a part of everyday life. Why do you think Noguchi wanted to get art out of museums and into parks and playgrounds? How does art affect your daily life?

UNDERSTANDING WORDS IN CONTEXT

Read the following sentences from the biography. Think about what each underlined word means. In your notebook, write what the word means as it is used in the sentence.

1. Many of Noguchi's most important designs are not found in museums. They are in places where people can be part of them. Some are stage sets for actors and dancers.

2. Soon after arriving [in Paris], Noguchi visited Brancusi's studio. The famed sculptor said that he did not accept students.

3. In winter, you can race your sled down a twisting, turning spiral.

4. In such a garden, every object is carefully chosen both for its physical beauty and its symbolic meaning. Even the space between objects is not seen as mere emptiness. The space is a "presence" with its own shape and importance.

5. In a 1968 interview [Noguchi] said, "I am the <u>fusion</u> of two worlds, the East and West. . . . Yet I hope I reflect more than both."

RECALLING DETAILS

1. What were the cultural backgrounds of Noguchi's mother and father?

2. Why did Noguchi change careers?

3. With what medium besides stone did Noguchi enjoy working? Why?

4. Describe Noguchi's sculpture in the Park of Peace in Hiroshima, Japan.

5. Why did Noguchi travel to Italy the year that he died?

UNDERSTANDING INFERENCES

In your notebook, write two or three sentences from the biography that support each of the following inferences.

1. Noguchi wanted people to feel a connection with his art.

2. Noguchi learned from others and respected the past.

3. Noguchi did not fear trying new ways to express himself through his art.

4. Noguchi was more concerned with practicing his art than with being successful.

5. Noguchi's Japanese heritage influenced his thinking and his art.

INTERPRETING WHAT YOU HAVE READ

1. How did Noguchi's time alone in the United States as a teenager influence him?

2. Why was Noguchi unhappy with his career until he discovered Brancusi's work?

3. How does Noguchi's sculpture for the dance *Cave of the Heart* make the dance more effective?

4. Choose one of Noguchi's works and explain its symbolism.

5. How is Noguchi's Japanese heritage reflected in the types of art he created?

ANALYZING QUOTATIONS

Read the following quotation from the biography and answer the questions below.

> *"I am the fusion of two worlds, the East and West. . . . Yet I hope I reflect more than both."*

1. What does the quotation suggest about Noguchi's feelings about himself?

2. In what ways do you think Isamu Noguchi's work combines the East and the West but reflects more than both?

3. What comes to mind when you think of the East and the West? Describe ways in which the two worlds might be blended.

THINKING CRITICALLY

1. Recall Noguchi's descriptions of how it felt to work with stone and clay. Why do his words seem so appropriate to someone who chose to be a sculptor?

2. What other careers might have appealed to Noguchi?

3. Why do you think Noguchi was uncomfortable about his success? Do you think his experiences with having his talent and work rejected affected his views about success? Explain.

4. You have learned about Noguchi as an artist. Choose three words that would describe Noguchi as a person. Explain your choices.

5. As a teenager, Isamu Noguchi was separated from his parents and had no "real" home, yet he turned these disadvantages into advantages. Do you know someone who has used challenging circumstances to his or her advantage? Explain.

MAYA LIN

Maya Lin, architect of the Vietnam Veterans Memorial, directs a
construction worker. The traditional values of her Chinese heritage,
including respect for the individual and nature, are often reflected
in Lin's designs.

Some homework assignments are more unusual than others. Maya Ying Lin's assignment was to design the Vietnam Veterans[1] Memorial. It was 1980, and Maya, a senior at Yale University, was just 21 years old. She was studying to be an architect.[2] In her class in funerary architecture—the design of buildings or monuments in memory of people who have died—the professor assigned all his students to enter the national competition.

The memorial[3] would honor the U.S. forces who had died in the Vietnam War, a war fought in the late 1960s and early 1970s, when Maya was still a child. She knew little about the two governments that had struggled to control Vietnam, a country in Southeast Asia. She did know, however, that feelings about the war had divided the United States. Some people thought the United States was right to send soldiers to help the government of South Vietnam. Others strongly disagreed.

Most of Lin's classmates began their work by learning more about the war. Maya chose another path. She went to the park in Washington, D.C., where the memorial was to be built. "I walked around this beautiful park, surrounded by trees," Maya wrote later. "I didn't want to destroy a living park. You use the landscape, you don't fight with it." As she looked at the grass, the trees, and the rise and fall of the land, a clear design for the memorial came to her. Maya pictured a V-shaped opening in the earth, an opening that would make a link "between the sunny world and the quiet, dark world beyond that we can't enter."

1. **veterans** (VEHT-uh-ruhnz) *n. pl.* people who have served in the armed services
2. **architect** (AHR-kuh-tehkt) *n.* a person whose profession is designing buildings, bridges, or other structures
3. **memorial** (muh-MOHR-ee-uhl) *n.* something meant to help people remember people or events

Instead of forcing a design onto the land, Maya let the land tell her what her design should be. She had learned this way of thinking from her parents and their Chinese culture. "My parents never forced us to do anything," she recalls. "Maybe that is an Eastern philosophy[4]—that you don't force an opinion on a child. You allow them to draw their own conclusions."

Maya's parents also gave her a belief in education and an appreciation of the arts. The Lins had left China in 1948, just before the Communists took over the country, and had moved to the United States. Both became teachers at Ohio University—her father taught fine arts and her mother taught Asian and English literature.

Maya was born in Athens, Ohio, in 1959. She and her older brother Tan grew up in "a glass-walled house in the woods." Their home was full of books and art, including her father's collection of ancient Chinese pottery. (See **Did You Know?** on page 77 for more information on Chinese pottery.) Maya learned early how to design and build things. Her father, Henry, a famous potterymaker, taught her to throw pots.[5] She also made simple sculptures and built little towns in her room. These were the first signs of her later interest in sculpture and architecture.

The contest attracted 1,420 other entries. Winning meant a $20,000 prize plus the attention of many powerful people. Maya Lin was sure that her entry would not win. She was young and inexperienced, and her design was "different." But all the judges agreed that Lin's design was the best.

Maya's design for the memorial seemed very simple. It was two black granite walls, each 250 feet long, that formed a "V." The walls started at ground level and gradually reached a height of 10 feet at their meeting point. The end of one wall pointed to the Lincoln Memorial, and the end of the other to the Washington Monument. The back of the memorial was buried

----

4. **philosophy** (fuh-LAHS-uh-fee) *n.* a person's, or a culture's, principles and beliefs

5. **throw pots** shape pottery on a potter's wheel

in the hill, but its "face" was open. The public was to approach it by going down a grassy slope.

Lin's design called for the names of the 58,000 people who died in the war to be carved in the dark wall. Typically, names on memorials are listed in alphabetical order, but Lin wanted them arranged by the order in which people died. This was a way of recording the history of the war. She wanted the names and the gentle landscape to speak for themselves.

Maya's father believed that his daughter's liking for simple designs came from the family's Chinese roots. "The quietness and the directness really is an Eastern influence," he once said. Maya agrees. The memorial, she explains, "does not force or dictate how you should think. . . . In that sense it's very Eastern—it says, 'This is what happened, these are the people'. . . . It reflects me and my parents."

Some veterans and art critics were angry when pictures of Maya's design appeared in the newspapers. One person called it "a black gash of shame." Others complained that its "V" shape was like the "peace sign" that many associated with people who opposed the war. Still others did not want a memorial designed by someone who had not participated in the war. Some veterans even attacked Maya because of her Asian ancestry. They saw all Asians as enemies.

Maya had to fight fiercely for her design as it was being built. Some people on the memorial committee thought her design was too abstract and untraditional. They voted to add a flag and a statue of soldiers to it. Maya insisted that these be placed near the entrance to the park, away from her black wall. She wanted to protect the simplicity of her statement, and she succeeded.

The memorial was dedicated[6] on Veterans Day 1982. Most people who attended the ceremony agreed with the evaluation in *The Washington Post:* "The argument over the memorial dissolves the moment you get there." Soldiers and their families walked slowly along the wings of the "V" or stood in the quiet space at

---

6. **dedicated** (DEHD-ih-kayt-uhd) *v.* opened formally to the public

its center. They touched the names. The reflection of their hands seemed to reach back toward them from the wall's dark depths. Some people left pictures, notes, and even medals. Many people simply cried. Today the Vietnam Veterans Memorial, or the "Wall" as many call it, attracts more visitors than any other monument in the United States.

The Wall was a victory, but Maya Lin did not enjoy being famous. The attacks on her design and on her as a person had shaken her. For a while she doubted her career choice and even dropped out of school. But later she returned, earning her Master's degree in architecture from Yale in 1986. Lin then began to work in both sculpture and architecture, often combining the two. "Architecture . . . is like writing a book," she says. "Everything in a building matters, from the doorknobs to the paint details. And sculpture is like writing a poem. You're not saying as much. It's an idea stripped bare."

Maya was certain she would never design another memorial. The process had been too painful. But then, in 1987, she got a phone call from Morris Dees, head of the Southern Poverty Law Center in Montgomery, Alabama. The Center wanted a memorial built to honor the struggle for African American civil rights[7] during the late 1950s and early 1960s. Dees and the other Center leaders knew that Maya Lin was the person to design the memorial. "We called every Lin in the New York telephone book until the right one answered," Dees said later.

Maya Lin soon agreed to design the memorial. She felt strongly about the Center's commitment to protect African American civil rights and to educate all Americans about their civil rights. "I'm really interested in a nation's memory and how art deals with a country's conscience,"[8] she explains. Maya began immediately to read about the Civil Rights Movement. She was

---

7. **civil rights** (SIHV-uhl REYETS) *n. pl.* rights guaranteed by the U.S. Constitution and other acts of Congress

8. **conscience** (KAHN-shuhnts) *n.* a knowledge or sense of right and wrong, with an urge to do right

still reading as a plane carried her to Montgomery in May 1988. Suddenly, part of a speech by civil rights leader Martin Luther King, Jr., caught her imagination: "We will not be satisfied until justice rolls down like waters and righteousness[9] like a mighty stream." Maya had found her theme. "I knew that the whole piece had to be about water," she said later.

Lin's Civil Rights Memorial, like the Vietnam Memorial, is made of shiny black granite. Part of it is a curving wall 9 feet high. King's words, beginning with *until,* are carved on the wall and water runs continually down its surface. The rest of the memorial is a round disk almost 12 feet across. Around the edge are dates and names positioned like the numbers on a sundial. The dates mark important events in the civil rights struggle, while the names belong to people who were killed in that struggle. A thin sheet of water flows over the disk. People's hands make ripples in the water as they touch the names and dates.

The Civil Rights Memorial was finished on November 5, 1989. The families of many of those whose names appear on the disk came to the dedication. One man's mother cried as she touched his name. "I realized her tears were becoming part of the memorial," Maya says.

Maya again declares she will do no more memorials. She is designing a topiary[10] park in Charlotte, North Carolina, and a huge hanging sculpture for the Pennsylvania Railroad Station in New York City. As much as Maya likes sculpture, though, she feels a strong pull to remain an architect, in part because she is a woman. "I'm determined to prove that women can get things built," she says. "If you are given the chance, you can change the rules and expectations."

Maya Lin has often changed rules and expectations during her working life. No doubt she will do so again. "I won't say it's

---

9. **righteousness** (REYE-chuhs-nuhs) *n.* the quality of being morally right or fair

10. **topiary** (TOH-pee-air-ee) *n.* the art of trimming and training shrubs into certain shapes, such as animals

going to be an easy route," she says of her career. "But . . . it's the only route I know to take. To me, design doesn't have to have straight lines."

Did You Know? *The interest that Maya Lin's father had in ancient Chinese pottery is shared by many scholars of Chinese history. Because stoneware originated in China, its development can be used as a time line throughout many periods in Chinese history. By studying pottery found in the ruins of ancient Chinese settlements, historians can determine exactly when the settlements were active and the kinds of techniques and tools they used. For example, a pot that stands on three legs and is reddish in color with black geometric designs comes from an earlier time than a pot that is shiny black and was created on a potter's wheel. With the coming of the Shang dynasty in China (1523-1028 B.C.), the Bronze Age began. Pottery was replaced by bronze.*

AFTER YOU READ

EXPLORING YOUR RESPONSES

1. Maya Lin's approach to designing the Vietnam Veterans Memorial was different from that of her classmates. Tell about a time when you or someone you know approached a task in a unique way.

2. Maya's parents "never forced us to do anything." Do you think parents should force their children to do things? Why?

3. Maya's father believed that her preference for simple designs comes from the family's Chinese background. Which of your interests can be traced to your family's background? Explain.

4. Many people opposed Lin's design, but she stood firm. Tell about a time at which you stood up for something you believed.

5. Lin wants to remain an architect, in part to prove that women can succeed in the profession. Tell about someone you admire who has helped others along by paving the way.

UNDERSTANDING WORDS IN CONTEXT

Read the following sentences from the biography. Think about what each underlined word means. In your notebook, write what the word means as it is used in the sentence.

1. The memorial would honor the U.S. forces who had died in the Vietnam War.

2. She was studying to be an architect. In her class in funerary architecture–the design of buildings or monuments in memory of people who have died–the professor assigned all students to enter the national competition.

3. "Maybe that is an Eastern philosophy–that you don't force an opinion on a child."

4. The memorial was dedicated on Veterans Day, 1982. Most people who attended the ceremony agreed with the

evaluation in *The Washington Post:* "The argument over the memorial dissolves the moment you get there."

5. "I'm really interested in a nation's memory and how art deals with a country's <u>conscience</u>."

RECALLING DETAILS

1. How did Maya prepare to design the Vietnam memorial?
2. List three words or phrases used in the biography to describe the Vietnam Veterans Memorial.
3. List some ways in which people reacted to the Vietnam Veterans Memorial and the Civil Rights Memorial.
4. Name three things that happened in Maya's life after the Vietnam memorial was built.
5. To what do the names and dates on the Civil Rights Memorial refer?

UNDERSTANDING INFERENCES

In your notebook, write two or three sentences from the biography that support each of the following inferences:

1. Art and literature were important influences in Maya Lin's life.
2. Lin's approach to design was influenced by her heritage.
3. Maya has not always enjoyed her fame.
4. Maya was wise to refuse to change her design.
5. Lin's Vietnam and civil rights memorials have a number of similarities.

INTERPRETING WHAT YOU HAVE READ

1. Maya's parents "never forced" anything on her. How does this relate to her design of the Vietnam memorial?
2. Why do you think many people criticized Maya's design?
3. In what way is either of the memorials Maya Lin designed symbolic? Be specific.

4. One mother cried when she touched her son's name on the Civil Rights Memorial. In what sense did her tears become part of the memorial?

5. When talking about her career, Lin says, "design doesn't have to have straight lines." What do you think she means?

ANALYZING QUOTATIONS

Read the following quotation from the story and answer the questions below.

> When talking about the Vietnam memorial, Maya says that it "does not force or dictate how you should think. . . . In that sense it's very Eastern—it says, 'This is what happened, these are the people.' . . . It reflects me and my parents."

1. In what sense is Maya's design for the Vietnam Veterans Memorial a reflection of her and her parents?

2. How do you think the Vietnam memorial might have looked if Lin wanted to tell people what to think?

3. Think about something you did recently that took effort and creativity—like writing a story, painting a picture, or preparing a meal. How does it reflect your family's attitudes and beliefs?

THINKING CRITICALLY

1. Why do you think Lin chose to learn more about the memorial's location than about the Vietnam War?

2. What kind of memorial do you think Maya's critics wanted?

3. If you could visit either one of Lin's memorials, which would you choose and why?

4. What characteristics might an architect and a sculptor share?

5. List some aspects of Lin's personality that helped her become successful. Then list some aspects of your personality that may help you become successful, too.

JOSÉ ARUEGO

José Aruego, Filipino American illustrator, draws upon his childhood
experiences in the Philippines for his illustrations. This book cover
reflects Aruego's sense of humor and love of animals.

As luck would have it, José Aruego's (hoh-SAY ahr-oo-AY-goh) first case was his last–legal case, that is. "I still cannot figure out why I took up law. I guess it was because my father is a lawyer, my sister is a lawyer, and all my friends went to law school. All my friends became very successful [businesspeople], lawyers, and politicians. They were all confused when they found out I was doing children's books," José once said.

Aruego's friends may have been confused when he suddenly became an illustrator, but the change should not have been so surprising. The signs of his drawing talent, love of humor, and feeling for animals were always there.

José Aruego was born in the Philippines in 1932. (See **Did You Know?** on page 86 for more information about the Philippines.) His father was a practicing lawyer who also taught law at the University of Manila. The whole family was involved in law and politics. Yet their house in Manila was a lively place, too, for a boy who liked to draw.

"I remember a time when we had three horses . . . seven dogs and their puppies, six or seven cats and their kittens, a backyard filled with chickens and roosters, a house of pigeons, frogs, tadpoles and ducks in our miniature rice paddies that had a lot of water lilies, and three very fat pigs that belonged to my sister. This was in our small house in the city," José recalled. "My childhood was kept in the company of animals."

Young José loved and collected comic books as well as animals. Perhaps he enjoyed comics because he himself was a doodler. Every chance he got, he doodled and drew, especially at school. The bulletin boards, the chalkboards–anywhere he could–he would practice drawing. "All kids, when young, like to draw," José concluded, "and if they are known for it, feel good." José thought that if he were good at drawing, people would take notice. But more importantly, he liked to please others. His drawings always seemed to do that.

Despite his interest in drawing, José followed the path that was laid out for him without asking questions. He enrolled in the University of the Philippines and took all the prescribed[1] pre-law courses. After earning a Bachelor of Arts degree in 1953, José went to law school. He got his law degree in 1955.

Not really interested in law, José did not study very much for the bar exam. Yet, he did pass—barely. At least he could go on to practice law in the family tradition.

It should have been an exciting time for Aruego to begin his legal career. The Republic of the Philippines had been granted independence from the United States on July 4, 1946. José's father had been active in the discussions that helped shape the new nation's constitution. The country was beginning to re-cover from World War II. In Manila, the capital city, banking, manufacturing, and trade were beginning to flourish.[2] Many opportunities awaited a well-educated young person.

The rookie[3] lawyer worked for less than three months, though, at his new profession. After he lost his first case, Aruego made the most important decision of his young life. He would follow his boyhood dream and become an artist.

To José's delight, his parents supported his decision. His father even encouraged him to go to Paris where many well-known artists worked and studied. José appreciated his father's suggestion, but there was someplace else he wanted to go—New York City, the comic book capital of the world.

In no time, José Aruego was off to the United States. There he enrolled in the Parsons School of Design. As much as he loved his art and design classes, however, living in a strange culture was a tough adjustment for him. "At first, I wanted to go

---

1. **prescribed** (prih-SKREYEBD) *adj.* ordered or established by a rule
2. **flourish** (FLER-ihsh) *v.* grow and prosper
3. **rookie** (ROOK-ee) *adj.* inexperienced

home right away; I had to adapt. I missed friends, family," José later recalled. After his first year in New York, life became easier.

At the end of his second year at Parsons, José spent the summer studying art in Europe. There he learned to make line drawings, or drawings that use lines made by pencil, pen, crayon, paintbrush, chalk, or charcoal. This technique particularly suited his talent. "I discovered that line drawing is a great fulfillment. I drew everything from fire extinguishers to Rodin[4] sculptures to drinking fountains," he remembers.

After graduating from Parsons with a certificate in graphic arts and advertising in 1959, Aruego took a job gluing feathers on the wings of angel mannequins.[5] But he was laid off right after Christmas. For the next six years, José held a variety of jobs, working for advertising agencies and magazines.

To meet other people, José joined the International House in New York City. As a member ambassador[6] for the organization's international friendship program, he traveled throughout the United States and to several other countries. It was at the International House that he met another artist, Ariane Dewey, whom he married in 1961.

Aruego was now drawing cartoons every chance he got—after work, before work, between jobs—and submitting them to magazines. After a while, his work was accepted by magazines such as the *Saturday Evening Post*, *Look*, and *The New Yorker*. As he sold more and more cartoons, his confidence increased.

Finally, José became a full-time freelance[7] cartoonist. As a freelancer, he worked alone, submitting his cartoons to many magazines at once. If a magazine printed his cartoon, he was paid. As exciting as it was to be published, however, the

---

4. **Rodin, Auguste** (roh-DAN) French sculptor who lived from 1840-1917; his most famous work is The Thinker

5. **mannequins** (MAN-ih-kihnz) *n. pl.* models of the human body used by dressmakers, window dressers, and artists

6. **ambassador** (am-BAS-uh-duhr) *n.* a special representative

7. **freelance** (FREE-lans) *adj.* independent, working on a project basis

rejections were discouraging. José once estimated that for every 20 cartoons he submitted, only one was accepted.

For more than two years, though, he stuck it out as a freelance cartoonist. At the same time, Aruego was writing and illustrating a children's book. The book, called *The King and His Friends*, was dedicated to his newborn son, Juan. Although rejected by one publisher, another children's book publisher, Charles Scribner's Sons, accepted it. An editor there was very impressed with José's illustrations. This book, the first of many illustrated by José Aruego, was published in 1969.

From that point on, José concentrated on children's books. His second book was published in 1970. He did the illustrations and Robert Kraus wrote the text. That book, called *Whose Mouse Are You?*, was selected as an American Library Association Notable Book.

In his second year as a writer and illustrator of children's books, José Aruego had five books published. One of them, *Juan and the Asuangs,* won the Outstanding Picture Book of the Year Award from *The New York Times*. In 1972, *A Crocodile's Tale*, on which he and his wife Ariane collaborated,[8] was published. The book won the praise of the Children's Book Council Showcase and the American Institute of Graphic Arts.

José Aruego's work has been hailed as brilliant, fresh, and bold. His line drawings are simple yet detailed, and his animal characters warmly amusing. Of his work, Aruego has said, "I have written mostly animal stories. The ideas must have humor. They must take off from something funny. If they are serious, I cannot get my juices working. Kids like to be happy, and my books give them the opportunity."

Aruego's debt to his heritage is clear. His studio is filled with plants and numerous objects from the Philippines. His stories contain images and ideas from Filipino stories that have been handed down over many generations. José's illustrations, too,

8. **collaborated** (kuh-LAB-u-ray-tihd) *v.* worked together

reflect his heritage and his roots in the tropical climate of the Philippines. "Someone told me my drawings are very tropical. The lines are like calligraphy[9] at home in the Philippines, and the background art is very decorative," the artist notes.

Aruego has returned often to the Philippines to visit friends and family. In 1976, he went for a very special reason. He had been named the Outstanding Filipino Abroad in Arts, and he made the journey to accept the award. "When I . . . went home, it was nice being recognized in my new profession," José admitted. "Lots of my lawyer classmates and professors were proud that I made it as an illustrator. I changed professions and changed to what is successful [for me]."

José continues to create enchanting, funny, zestful[10] creatures and stories, often working on several books at a time. But he also finds time to visit schools to talk to young people about his work. What advice can José Aruego offer would-be artists? "If you intend drawing as your profession, you must be ready to compromise. . . . You cannot always do what you want. In the beginning, you have to adjust your style to earn money. Do what you want on the side. The most beautiful thing is doing what you want when that earns money." Of the future, Aruego says simply, "This is what I will be doing for quite some time. Hopefully, people like my work. It is what I want to do."

> **Did You Know?** *The culture of the Republic of the Philippines contains a mixture of Asian and European influences. The Spanish ruled the 7,000 islands that make up the Philippines for more than 300 years. As a result, most of the people, like José Aruego, have Spanish names. Filipinos, however, do not speak Spanish. The country's official languages are English and Pilipino.*

---

9. **calligraphy** (kuh–LIHG–ruh–fee) *n.* beautiful, artistic handwriting
10. **zestful** (ZEHST–ful) *adj.* anything stimulating, exciting, or full of energy

AFTER YOU READ

EXPLORING YOUR RESPONSES

1. If you were writing a children's book, what characters or situations might you include?

2. Humor is very important to Aruego's work. Name another writer who uses humor and describe what you like about that writer's work.

3. Aruego's cartoons were often rejected. If you had been his friend, how might you have helped him through this difficult time?

4. "My childhood was kept in the company of animals," the artist recalls. Why do you think animals can often be good companions for people?

5. One reason José Aruego went into law was that all his friends became lawyers and businesspeople. When do you think peer pressure can have a good effect? When can it become bad?

UNDERSTANDING WORDS IN CONTEXT

Read the following sentences from the biography. Think about what each underlined word means. In your notebook, write what the word means as it is used in the selection.

1. He enrolled in the University of the Philippines, and took all the prescribed pre-law courses.

2. In Manila, the capital city, banking, manufacturing, and trade were beginning to flourish. Many opportunities awaited a well-educated young professional.

3. The rookie lawyer worked less than three months, though, at his new profession.

4. Finally, José became a full-time freelance cartoonist. As a freelancer, he worked alone.

5. In 1972, *A Crocodile's Tale,* on which he and his wife Ariane <u>collaborated</u>, was published.

RECALLING DETAILS

1. Describe José's childhood home and activities.

2. What did Aruego do while he was in Europe?

3. Describe José's law career.

4. Why did Aruego want to go to New York?

5. How did Aruego make a living after he left Parsons?

UNDERSTANDING INFERENCES

In your notebook, write two or three sentences from the biography that support each of the following inferences.

1. José's trip to Europe helped him to develop his artistic abilities.

2. Certain childhood experiences shaped Aruego's later life.

3. For young Aruego, life in New York was quite different from life in the Philippines.

4. Aruego's career as an artist has had its up and downs.

5. José Aruego loves animals and children.

INTERPRETING WHAT YOU HAVE READ

1. José Aruego went into law even though he preferred art. What does this tell you about his relationship with his family?

2. How do you think José felt about losing his first legal case?

3. Why do you think comic books had a strong influence on the young artist?

4. How did Aruego adjust to his life in New York?

5. How does José Aruego's art reflect his feelings about animals?

ANALYZING QUOTATIONS

Read the following quotation from the selection and answer the questions that follow.

> "I have written mostly animal stories. The ideas must have humor. They must take off from something funny. If they are serious, I cannot get my juices working. Kids like to be happy, and my books give them the opportunity."

1. What does the quotation tell you about Aruego's approach to his work?
2. Why do you think the artist might use animals in his stories?
3. If you were to write or draw something to make children happy, what would it be?

THINKING CRITICALLY

1. Why do you think José Aruego chose to be an artist?
2. How might Aruego's life have been different if he had not gone to law school?
3. Aruego has said many times, in many ways, "Enjoy your work." What role does personal satisfaction play in career success? In relationships?
4. How important has recognition been to Aruego? Explain.
5. What impact has José's Philippine background had on his art? In what ways might someone's heritage affect his or her future?

CONNIE CHUNG

Connie Chung, anchor for CBS TV news, sits at the network's news desk. In 1987, Chung conducted a live broadcast from China, where she was reunited with relatives. Chung says that this experience helped define her cultural identity.

What does it take to become a national "news anchor," the face that millions of people see when they turn on their television for the evening news? What lies behind the well-groomed, self-assured image on the screen?

The career of Connie Chung (CHUNG), a Chinese American TV journalist[1] and news anchor, provides an answer to these questions. Her rise to the top of a very competitive profession is not a "Cinderella" story, though. Chung worked hard at her craft for many years and made many personal sacrifices to become the respected broadcaster she is. Described by news anchor Dan Rather as "a nuclear reactor of energy," Chung has helped change the way people see women—and Asian Americans—in the television industry.

Constance Yu-hwa Chung was born in Washington, D.C., on August 20, 1946. She was the youngest of ten children, although five of her brothers and sisters had died in China during World War II. Her father, William Ling Chung, was a diplomat[2] in the Nationalist Chinese government. However, in 1945, as the Chinese Communists grew more powerful, William Chung arranged to be transferred to the Chinese embassy[3] in Washington, D.C. He later became a successful businessperson, and he and his wife, Margaret, raised their five remaining daughters in a Washington suburb.

When Connie was born, one year after her family emigrated to the United States, William Chung gave her sisters the job of naming her. Connie laughs as she describes what happened:

1. **journalist** (JER-nuhl-ihst) *n.* a person who gathers, writes, edits, and reports the news

2. **diplomat** (DIHP-luh-mat) *n.* a person who handles negotiations between nations

3. **embassy** (EHM-buh-see) *n.* the office of the representatives of a foreign country

"They went to their movie magazines and said, 'O.K., the first page we turn to is going to be her.' It could have been a real disaster," Connie exclaims, "but it was Constance Moore.[4] Oh, was I lucky."

Connie Chung's later ease in the spotlight would have been hard to predict when she was growing up. She was shy and quiet. She felt intimidated[5] by her older sisters. A vivid childhood memory sums up her painful shyness. One of Connie's elementary school teachers wrote "speaks too softly" on her report card. Connie remembers being very hurt and crying all the way home from school.

In her teens, however, Connie started learning to express herself. She appeared in school plays and variety shows. She also became interested in student government and in politics generally. As Connie once told an interviewer: "You can't grow up in Washington, D.C. . . . without developing an interest for how this country works."

After spending two years at the University of Maryland studying biology, Connie worked as a summer intern[6] for Seymour Halpern, a Representative from New York. Part of her job was writing speeches and press releases, or information for the news media. Connie discovered that she enjoyed writing very much and soon switched her major[7] to journalism.

During this period, Connie also worked part-time for WTTG, a local TV station, as a clerical assistant. When she graduated from college, Connie was promoted to a secretarial job in the news department. She showed her interest in journalism, though, by volunteering to do research and to help write news stories for the anchorperson. When Connie knew that no one

---

4. **Constance Moore** (MOHR) U.S. stage and screen actress during the late 1930s through the late 1940s

5. **intimidated** (ihn-TIHM-uh-dayt-uhd) *adj.* frightened or timid

6. **intern** (IHN-tuhrn) *n.* a student gaining experience in a job by working with a professional

7. **major** (MAY-juhr) *n.* the area of study in which a student specializes

was covering a story, she offered to go out to get the news herself.

Soon Connie was promoted to news writer, often covering stories as an on-air reporter. Some of these stories, such as murders and airplane crashes, could be pretty grim. "It was quite a shock for a girl from a sheltered Chinese home, but I'd plow through and get there anyway."

While covering stories of national significance, Chung met major network reporters. Impressed by their knowledge and experience, she soon wanted to move on to the wider, more challenging world of national network news. In 1971 her chance came. The networks knew that they had to hire more minorities and women, in part to satisfy viewer demand and government requirements. Connie was one of four women reporters hired by CBS News that year. One of her first assignments—covering Senator George McGovern's campaign for the presidency—showed that CBS believed in her ability.

Soon after, Chung gained experience in foreign affairs when she accompanied President Richard Nixon on trips to the Middle East and the Soviet Union in the early 1970s. She also used her Chinese language skills to help prepare stories about the President's historic trip to Beijing (bay-JING), the capital of China, though she herself would not visit China for several years.

Most reporters can name "the big story" that changed the course of their life. For Connie Chung, that story is the Watergate scandal, which unfolded in 1973 and 1974. Watergate is the name given to a political scandal involving Richard Nixon, who was the President of the United States at that time. Uncovering the crimes of high government officials both educated and challenged her. "To me, Watergate was the story of the decade. It was the unraveling of the Presidency, a textbook course in responsible reporting and a lesson in truth. . . . I felt the weight and responsibility to be fair and accurate because we were dealing with the future of the Presidency of the United States. I developed a standard for myself."

By 1976, Chung was eyeing the top job in any TV news operation—the news anchor. A station's ratings, or popularity, often depend on the success of this person. Connie had enough experience to know that the anchor's job is not as glamorous as it appears. The deadlines[8] of TV news are measured not in weeks or months but in hours or even minutes. The business also involves intense competition among reporters for status[9] and better assignments. Nevertheless, Connie wanted to try.

Before long, she won the job of co-anchor at KNXT, a local CBS station in Los Angeles. By 1983, Connie Chung was earning about $600,000 a year, making her the highest paid local TV anchor in the country, but it was time for a change. After seven years at KNXT, Chung left Los Angeles and CBS for a position as anchor of *NBC News at Sunrise* and the Saturday *NBC Nightly News.*

Sometimes going forward means taking a few steps back. Moving from prime time to a less popular time, even at the national level, meant that Chung had to accept a considerable cut in pay. On the other hand, she would gain experience and reach many more viewers.

In 1987, Chung was part of an NBC news team that broadcast live from China. While on tour, she was reunited with relatives and even interviewed some of them on air. For her it was "the most rewarding experience I ever had. They had a story to tell, and through their experience, they told the history of modern China—how the war affected this family, how the Cultural Revolution had affected that family. I went to my grandparents' graves . . . and I cried a lot with my relatives. I think it was meaningful to the viewers, because it was *my* family. My life has been much more defined by my roots since that experience." (See **Did You Know?** on page 95 for more information on the Cultural Revolution.)

Working in the fast-paced world of TV news can make it hard to have a normal family life. While working in Los

---

8. **deadlines** (DEHD-leyenz) *n. pl.* the times by which things must be done
9. **status** (STAT-uhs) *n.* position or rank in relation to others

Angeles, Connie met Maury Povitch, a successful TV personality who was for a time her co-anchor and later hosted *A Current Affair* on Fox Television. They dated for several years and were married in 1984.

As Connie Chung works to build a rewarding private life, her career keeps moving forward. In 1989, she left NBC and went back to CBS to anchor various programs. By that time, though, the news reporter was making news with her salary of more than $1 million a year. In 1993, she once again made news by becoming co-anchor with Dan Rather of the CBS evening news.

Connie Chung has advice for anyone thinking about a career in broadcast journalism: "Don't be quick to get on the air and anchor. Learn to write. Sit down and write for someone else or for print. It's the greatest way to organize your thoughts and learn to tell a story clearly. If you write well, you can do anything in this business, in television news or in print journalism." Chung's success is proof that learning the basics can make all the difference.

> **Did You Know?** *In the spring and summer of 1966, Mao Zedong (MOW dzuh-DOONG), who was the Chairman of the Communist party in China, believed that some members of Chinese society were becoming too privileged. He called on the youth of China to establish a new kind of Chinese society. Millions of high school and college students left their classrooms and formed a military-like group called the Red Guards. The Red Guards targeted anyone who seemed too privileged—professors, factory managers, and government officials. Independent thinking was punished; educated people were made to work menial jobs. More than 20 years later, Connie Chung, the daughter of immigrants who fled communism, depends on the open exchange of ideas in order to fully inform the public.*

AFTER YOU READ

EXPLORING YOUR RESPONSES

1. Connie changed her major from biology to writing. How does a person decide on a career? Use examples from the lives of people you know or about whom you have read.

2. Connie Chung sometimes chose to take a cut in pay or status to achieve a long-term goal. If you were in her place, what might you have done?

3. Chung created her own opportunities. How might you create opportunities for yourself? Be specific.

4. Connie pushed herself to get the news. Give examples of other careers in which a person has to work hard at difficult tasks to be successful.

5. Connie achieved national prominence after many years of hard work. Think of a career goal you have. Then list five steps you might take to achieve that goal.

UNDERSTANDING WORDS IN CONTEXT

Read the following sentences from the biography. Think about what each underlined word means. In your notebook, write what the word means as it is used in the sentence.

1. Her father, William Ling Chung, was a diplomat in the Nationalist Chinese government.

2. However, in 1945, as the Chinese Communists grew more powerful, William Chung arranged to be transferred to the Chinese embassy in Washington, D.C.

3. She was shy and quiet. She felt intimidated by her older sisters.

4. After spending two years at the University of Maryland studying biology, Connie worked as a summer intern for Seymour Halpern, a Representative from New York.

5. The business also involves intense competition among reporters for <u>status</u> and better assignments.

RECALLING DETAILS

1. Why did Connie Chung's family move to the United States?

2. As a child, why did Connie seem an unlikely person to become a TV personality?

3. What did Chung learn from her "big story"?

4. What were some of Connie Chung's accomplishments in her first anchor job?

5. Describe Chung's experiences in China.

UNDERSTANDING INFERENCES

In your notebook, write two or three sentences from the biography that support each of the following inferences.

1. Connie Chung's family experienced hardships in China.

2. Chung is not afraid of new experiences or of taking risks.

3. Becoming a TV anchorperson takes preparation and hard work.

4. Advancing her career has been more important to Connie than always seeking a high salary.

5. Chung's Chinese heritage is important to her.

INTERPRETING WHAT YOU HAVE READ

1. In high school Connie participated in school plays and student government. How might these experiences have helped prepare her for television broadcasting?

2. How did growing up in Washington, D.C., affect Connie's career?

3. Why did Connie leave her job in 1983 as CBS anchor in Los Angeles to take a lower paying job with NBC?

4. How is Connie Chung's career similar to that of her father?

5. Connie has met many important people in her career, but meeting her relatives in China moved her the most. Why?

ANALYZING QUOTATIONS

Read the following quotation from the biography and answer the questions below.

> *When Connie Chung was reunited with some of her relatives in China, she said, "My life has been much more defined by my roots since that experience."*

1. What do you think it means to be "defined" by your roots?

2. What does the quotation tell you about Chung's attitude toward her heritage both before and after the trip to China?

3. Do you think understanding your heritage might help you better understand yourself? Why or why not?

THINKING CRITICALLY

1. How do you think the family's history influenced Chung's life and career?

2. In 1971 the networks were actively looking for women and minority reporters. What qualities did Connie bring to her job besides her gender and cultural background?

3. Connie says that covering the Watergate scandal was for her "a textbook course in responsible reporting and a lesson in truth." What does this tell you about the difficulties and responsibilities of journalism?

4. Connie says that writing is "the greatest way to organize your thoughts." Explain the relationship between writing and news reporting.

5. Name one characteristic of Chung's personality that impresses you. What might readers find impressive about you? Why?

I.M. PEI

I.M. Pei, Chinese American architect, unveils his model of the
Rock 'n' Roll Hall of Fame to George V. Voinovich, mayor of
Cleveland, Ohio. The building will be built on the banks of the
Cuyahoga River in downtown Cleveland.

As a child, I. M. Pei (PAY) enjoyed playing in the countryside near his family's vacation home outside of Guangzhou (gooang-JOH), China. The place was called the Garden of the Lion Forest. The garden itself was like a work of art. Its peace and harmony made a lasting impression on the young boy, who grew up to become a famous architect.[1] (See **Did You Know?** on page 104 for more information on Chinese gardens.) His love of nature and respect for the environment continue to influence his work. Pei noted years later as he talked about one project, "When you are confronted with nature, you just don't try to compete with it. You try to join with it."

Ieoh (EYE-OH) Ming Pei, who is called I. M., was born in China in 1917. One of five children, I. M. was the eldest son. His father was a manager for the Bank of China. "The Chinese father-son relationship was based on respect," Pei explained, adding that his father, "was not the sort of man to pat a son on the head, or hug a daughter." Though his father expected him to go into banking, Pei was not interested. "I had seen from my father's experience that bankers were constantly under political pressure." Banking was not for him.

I. M. found his calling early in life, almost by accident. As a young student, he attended school in Shanghai where he worked and studied hard. I. M. was fascinated with the drama that was unfolding across the street from the movie theater a 23-story modern hotel being built in Shanghai. At the time, it was the tallest building in China. I. M. was impressed with the design of the Western-style building. He decided to become an architect.

Pei began to think about college. He spent hours in the library, looking through college catalogs. His father expected him

---

1. **architect** (AHR-kuh-tehkt) *n.* person who designs buildings

to go to Europe to study, as was the custom for many sons of well-to-do Chinese families in Shanghai. In a bold move, Pei announced his choice: the University of Pennsylvania in Philadelphia. "It was the descriptions of the architecture classes at Penn that did it," Pei said years later. So in 1935, at the age of 17, he set off for the United States to study.

After only two weeks at Penn, the aspiring[2] architect began to think his goal was out of reach. He saw some impressive drawings done by other students. He decided that the other students' artistic talents were far better than his own: "I was crushed. How, I thought, could I, with no artistic training, become an architect if I had to go up against such things?" Immediately he transferred to the Massachusetts Institute of Technology (M.I.T.) to study engineering. I. M.'s self-confidence may have been shaken, but the teaching staff at M.I.T. saw his design talent. They persuaded him to switch back to architecture. In 1940, I. M. graduated from M.I.T. with many honors and architectural awards.

Meanwhile, I. M. had met Eileen Loo, also from China, who had attended Wellesley College, near Boston. They were married in the spring of 1942, and both enrolled in the Graduate School of Design at Harvard University.

In the next few years, Pei studied and worked with some of the most talented U.S. and European architects of the time. He and Eileen also began their family. Eventually, they would have three sons and a daughter.

Pei's professional turning point came in 1948. A successful real estate developer from New York City offered I. M. a job. William Zeckendorf wanted the promising architect to work for him. It was unusual for a developer to have an architect on staff. Developers were sometimes viewed simply as salespeople—not creative types. In the job interview, as Pei later remembered, "It was clear that we were complete opposites." Zeckendorf, however, had a love for architecture. Though I. M. had some doubts, he took the job.

2. **aspiring** (uh-speyer-ihng) *adj.* reaching for a high goal

The two men developed a close working relationship. Zeckendorf provided I. M. with business experiences and challenges. From Zeckendorf, Pei learned that architects had to be good businesspeople, too. He also learned to be a salesperson, which meant he learned the art of negotiation.[3]

In 1955, the year he became a U.S. citizen, Pei formed his own company. The firm continued to work mainly for Zeckendorf, but Pei was becoming unhappy with his role. He ran the business while his staff did most of the design work. But the design was the fun part, as I. M. saw it. He stated later, "Design is something you have to put your hand to. . . . I felt trapped in the role of looking for jobs. . . . While my people had the luxury of doing one job at a time, I had to keep track of the whole enterprise. My growth as a designer was stunted. . . . In a way, Zeckendorf's financial problems were the beginning of my opportunity as an architect."

I. M. Pei ended his work with the developer. It wasn't easy to get that many good jobs at first. His reputation as a developer's architect was a disadvantage. But the opportunity to prove his design talent finally came along.

The National Center for Atmospheric Research was looking for an architect to design a weather research center in Colorado. The scientific research center would be the most up-to-date laboratory of its kind. Yet it was important that the center fit in with the mountain environment. Many talented architects were considered, but Pei was the unanimous choice because of his record at M.I.T. and at Harvard.

The center was to be built in a wilderness area just outside of Boulder, Colorado. Such a building in such a location was a challenge. Pei admitted, "It wasn't something I could jump right into. I had to start from scratch." Starting from scratch meant getting to know the area and the site, as well as the needs of the scientists.

---

3. **negotiation** (nih-goh-shee-AY-shuhn) *n.* discussing or bargaining to reach an agreement

Working on the research center set the style that was to become Pei's trademark.[4] He threw himself into the project. He wanted to know everything he could about how the center would be used. He wanted to understand the environment all around the center. I. M. and the director of the center talked for hours about the scientific research that would be carried out there. Repeatedly, I. M. hiked all around the site. He even slept in a sleeping bag on the ground to experience the place at night. Sleeping on the mountain, under the stars, he came to understand the place. He loved the beauty of the landscape, and he respected it.

Pei's inspiration came at last when he and Eileen visited Mesa Verde National Park in southwestern Colorado. He saw a harmonious[5] beauty in the ancient cliff dwellings[6] there. "Here it is, a work of architecture that is at peace with nature!" I. M. declared excitedly. His final design for the research center was a collection of buildings that seemed to grow out of their surroundings, much as the cliff dwellings in Mesa Verde did. Every effort was made to respect the environment, to join with it. Crushed stone from the foothills nearby was mixed with the concrete so that the color of the buildings would blend with the beautiful mountains. Even the road to the center was planned carefully. The center made an important and bold design statement. People saw it as a work of art.

Now more and more creative challenges came to Pei—university buildings, city halls, libraries, museums, housing and office complexes. Each project was different, but one after another, they won design awards. Just as it seemed that I. M. had become a

4. **trademark** (TRAYD-mahrk) *n.* a distinctive quality or feature that identifies a particular person or thing

5. **harmonious** (hahr-MOH-nee-uhs) *adj.* arranged in an orderly and pleasing way

6. **cliff dwellings** apartments with many stories that were built about a thousand years ago under overhanging cliffs by Native Americans in what is now the southwestern United States

superstar, however, disaster struck. The new John Hancock building in Boston was a sleek, slender skyscraper, designed by one of I. M.'s partners. During the construction, the large sheets of glass that formed the "skin" around the structure began to blow off. Fortunately, no one was hurt, but the effect on Pei and his firm was "immeasurable," I. M. said. The public's confidence was shaken for a time, but I. M. stood fast, defending his partner and the firm. "Going through this trial toughened us. It helped to cement us as partners; we did not give up on each other."

In the last few years, Pei has taken on some challenges, such as the Rock and Roll Hall of Fame. "When the committee . . . asked me to design the building, I was taken aback," Pei admitted. "But the people on the committee said that it didn't matter that I wasn't yet a fan, and I was greatly encouraged. And so I started my musical education."

The 70-year-old designer's education included listening to tapes of Elvis Presley, the Beatles, the Grateful Dead, Bob Dylan, Chuck Berry, the Supremes, and Fats Domino. "I had to know what rock and roll was," Pei explained. "I found all the music quite remarkable. . . . It was fascinating."

In the early 1990s, I.M. decided to slow down a bit and spend more time with his family. Though still quite active, he does take time to reflect on his career. For what would I. M. Pei like to be remembered? "I'd like to be known, really, as an architect of my time. . . . That's all and nothing more."

> **Did You Know?** *Chinese and Western gardens differ in important ways. Western gardeners insist on controlling their environment—their gardens are built to be like outdoor rooms. The Chinese believe that they share the world with the sky, mountains, water, and rocks. As a result, the Chinese have great respect for nature and take great pleasure in being outdoors in the countryside. The Chinese garden traditions were more than a thousand years old by the time I. M. Pei played in his family's countryside home.*

AFTER YOU READ

EXPLORING YOUR RESPONSES

1. I. M. said that his relationship with his father "was based on respect." How important do you think respect is in a parent-child relationship?

2. I. M. was able to learn something about U.S. culture from watching U.S. movies. How has a movie or television show influenced your life?

3. Pei and William Zeckendorf were said to be "complete opposites." Do you think it can be a good idea for "opposites" to work together? Explain.

4. For Pei, designing the East Building of the National Gallery of Art was the opportunity of a lifetime. What kind of opportunity would you consider the "chance of a lifetime"?

5. Pei stood by his partners during the difficulties with the John Hancock project. During what kinds of experiences do you think it is important for partners, or friends, to stick together?

UNDERSTANDING WORDS IN CONTEXT

Read the following sentences from the biography. Think about what each underlined word means. In your notebook, write what the word means as it is used in the sentence.

1. I. M. was impressed with the design of the Western-style building. He decided to become an architect.

2. After only two weeks at Penn, the aspiring architect began to think his goal was out of reach.

3. [Pei] also learned to be a salesperson, which meant he learned the art of negotiation.

4. Working on the research center set the style that was to become Pei's trademark.

5. He saw a <u>harmonious</u> beauty in the ancient cliff dwellings there. "Here it is, a work of architecture that is at peace with nature!" I. M. declared excitedly.

RECALLING DETAILS

1. Why did Pei transfer to M.I.T.?
2. How did William Zeckendorf influence Pei's career?
3. In what ways did I. M. prepare to design the National Center for Atmospheric Research?
4. How did the John Hancock building project affect Pei's career?
5. How did I. M. react when the Rock and Roll Hall of Fame Foundation asked him to design its building?

UNDERSTANDING INFERENCES

In your notebook, write two or three sentences from the biography that support each of the following inferences.

1. After he arrived at the University of Pennsylvania, Pei was unsure of his abilities.
2. The cliff dwellings at Mesa Verde had a strong influence on Pei's ideas about design.
3. I. M. Pei was good at selling his design abilities.
4. Pei could show courage in the face of trouble.
5. Though I. M. valued his Chinese heritage, he felt strong ties to the United States.

INTERPRETING WHAT YOU HAVE READ

1. I. M.'s father wanted him to study in Europe, not the United States. What does this tell you about his father's view of education?
2. Why did I. M. study architecture in the United States?

3. I. M. thought that if he couldn't draw, he probably couldn't be an architect. Was he right? Why or why not?

4. Why do you think the problems with the Hancock building were harmful to I.M. Pei's reputation?

5. How would you describe Pei's approach to a design problem?

ANALYZING QUOTATIONS

Read the following quotation from the biography and answer the questions below.

"When you are confronted with nature, you just don't try to compete with it. You try to join with it."

1. Why was I. M. concerned about the natural surroundings of a site?

2. In what ways do people sometimes "compete with nature"?

3. Have you ever seen a building or structure that seemed to join with its natural surroundings? If you have, describe it. If you haven't, describe how you would change a structure you have seen to help it blend with nature better.

THINKING CRITICALLY

1. How might I. M. Pei's childhood experiences have affected the way he designs buildings?

2. Why do you think I. M. Pei was a successful architect?

3. Why do you think Pei took the job with William Zeckendorf?

4. I. M. Pei chose a profession in which one's successes and failures are public. What characteristics would help a person succeed as an architect?

5. Throughout his professional life, I. M. had the support of his wife, Eileen. What kind of support do you look for from family members or friends?

UNIT 2

CULTURAL CONNECTIONS

Thinking About What People Do

1. Choose one of the people from this unit you would like to interview. In your notebook, write five interview questions and the answers you think that person might offer.

2. With a partner, choose one of the subjects in this unit. Write a short skit in which one of you is the subject's parent and the other is the subject. In your skit, have your "characters" act out an important event or turning point in the subject's life. Present your skit to the class.

3. Imagine that you are one of the subjects in this unit. You have been asked to give a talk in your native land (or your parents' homeland) telling students there why you choose to live in the United States. Give your speech to your class.

Thinking About Culture

1. In what ways did the parents of three of these subjects influence their child's life? Give examples.

2. How are the parent–child relationships portrayed in this unit similar and how are they different? Give examples from three of the selections.

3. Several of the subjects in this unit changed their minds about what work they wanted to do. Describe the similarities and differences between two of them.

4. What kinds of challenges and frustrations did these subjects face because of their cultural heritage? In what ways was their heritage an advantage?

Building Research Skills

Work with a partner to complete the following activity.

Choose two of the people discussed in this unit who you think have similar character traits. Prepare a list of questions about their similarities and differences. Your questions might include:

Hint: The Bibliography at the back of this book lists articles and books to help you begin your research.

☆ What experiences have the two people shared?

☆ What differences do you see between them?

Hint: Use your library's card catalog or computer data base to find books about the people you have chosen.

☆ How are their cultural heritages similar and different?

☆ How were their childhoods similar and different?

☆ How were their adjustments to U.S. culture similar and different?

Hint: Remember to support your ideas with examples from the biographies and from your research.

Next, go to the library to do research on the people you have chosen.

Write a short essay in which you compare and contrast the two people you have researched. Using your list of questions and making a Venn diagram may help guide your writing. Then present your essay orally to the class.

Extending Your Studies

VISUAL ARTS **Your task:** *To make a banner in a style of calligraphy.* Written language is central to the preservation of Asian culture. In fact, in China, the word for culture, *wen-hua,* means "to learn to read and write." Calligraphy is the art of beautiful handwriting and is valued highly in many Asian cultures. Each written character represents an entire word or syllable and is created with careful and fine brush strokes. In English calligraphy each character is a letter of the alphabet.

Look for instructional books on calligraphy in the library. Think of a phrase that is meaningful to you, then use an Asian or English style of calligraphy to write your phrase on a banner. Decorate your classroom or hallway with your banners. If your banner is in an Asian calligraphy, include a translation into English.

MATH **Your task:** *To make a class chart that identifies geometric elements in the buildings or sculptures in your community.* As an architect, Maya Lin must understand how the pieces of buildings fit together. To do this, she uses the principles of geometry. Use your math book or ask your math teacher to help you define these geometric terms:

☆ acute angle

☆ right angle

☆ obtuse angle

☆ straight angle

Now watch for these angles in the buildings or sculptures in your community. You might also research library books on sculpture or browse through a local art museum. If possible, visit or find a picture of the Vietnam Veterans Memorial in Washington, D.C. Which angle does the monument make?

Bring to class photographs or newspaper or magazine clippings that display the angles you have found and assemble them into a class chart of geometric elements.

SOCIAL STUDIES **Your task:** *To make a collage about tropical rain forests.* In José Aruego's biography, you learned that the Philippine Islands have a tropical climate. Where are the tropical areas of the world located? Study a globe and locate the equator. Now look above the equator and find the Tropic of Cancer. Look below the equator and locate the Tropic of Capricorn. The areas within these two lines, known as the tropics, are covered with many kinds of forests, including rain forests.

Work with a small group to learn more about tropical rain forests. To begin, find answers to these questions:

☆ Which country and continent has the largest share of rain forests?

☆ What is the average temperature in a rain forest?

☆ What kinds of plants and animals live in rain forests?

☆ Why are the rain forests being cut down?

☆ What can you do to protect the rain forests?

Assemble the facts and illustrations you have found. Make a group list of the ten most important facts about rain forests. Then compare your lists and illustrations with those of other groups and make a class collage that features 15 Facts About Rain Forests. Display your collage to inform other students about rain forests and what they might do to help save them.

WRITING WORKSHOP

As you know, a biography is the true story of a person's life. In this lesson, you will write a **biographical sketch of someone you know**–a classmate or someone your own age. Since your biography will be a sketch, do not try to cover the person's entire life. Just think about one event or situation that shows what this person is like. Then write your sketch to introduce your subject to the class.

PREWRITING

Begin your biographical sketch by selecting a friend or a classmate with whom you have shared an experience. Choose someone who interests you and who you feel would interest others.

Select a subject: Think about friends you have at school or in your neighborhood. In a notebook, jot down three or four names and something about each person–what you find most interesting or appealing–and two or three things the two of you have done together. Then, select the person who stands out the most.

Choose a focus: After you decide on a subject, you need to choose the event you will describe. (To help select an event, look through photographs of the two of you, or discuss with your friend the experiences you have listed.) The event should be one you remember well and that was important to you.

List details: After you choose an event, list all the details you can that describe the event, the person, and what you learned from that event. Brainstorm, that is, write whatever comes to mind without trying to form sentences. Ask yourself these questions:

☆ What happened?

☆ Where did the event take place?

☆ How did the place look?

☆ What sounds did you hear?

☆ What did your subject say and do?

☆ How did he or she react?

☆ How do you think the person felt?

☆ What did the event tell you about your subject?

☆ What did the event tell you about yourself?

As you write down your thoughts, use specific details to draw a clear picture of your subject.

Organizing: Now that you have chosen a subject and taken notes, you can begin to organize your material. In your notebook, write your friend's name, the event, the place it occurred, and what you learned from the event. (Your ideas may change as you write. Part of the fun of writing is being surprised.) For example:

Person: Marta
Event and place: Her 13th birthday party at Cabrillo Park.
What I learned: Friends can change but still remain friends.

DRAFTING

Once your ideas are organized, you can begin drafting the sketch.

The Opening: The opening should introduce the person and event you are writing about as well as hold the reader's interest. For example:

> *Marta thought that this was going to be her best birthday party ever. After all, she was going to be a teenager. What better way to begin than with a cookout at Cabrillo Park on the Fourth of July?*

The Body: Here you will bring your friend to life through your description of the event. Remember, however, that it is not the event you are portraying, but the person. By showing what your friend says and does, and how he or she looks, thinks, and feels, you let the reader "meet" your friend. Use the details you wrote when you were brainstorming to draw a clear picture of your friend.

The Closing: By the end of your sketch, the reader should be able to "see" your friend and understand what you learned from the event. In our example, the writer learned that friends can change but still remain friends.

> *As the fireworks exploded, the sky lit up as if it were noon. To my surprise, Marta grabbed my hand. "Isn't it awesome!" she screamed, jumping up and down as she had every Fourth of July since we were 6. Maybe some things never change.*

REVISING

Put your biographical sketch aside for a day or two. Then, with the help of another student who will act as your editor, evaluate and revise your work. See the directions for writers and student editors below.

Directions for Writers: Before giving your sketch to your classmate to edit, check it yourself. As you read, ask yourself these questions:

☆ Does the opening hold the reader's interest?

☆ Do I give enough details to describe the event?

☆ Am I *showing*, not *telling*, the reader what happened?

☆ Does the dialogue sound natural?

☆ Does the ending sum up what I learned and leave the reader with a lasting impression?

Make notes for your next draft or revise your work before you give it to a student editor. Then ask the student editor to read your work. Listen carefully to his or her suggestions. If they seem helpful, use them to improve your writing when you revise your work.

Directions for Student Editors: Read the work carefully and respectfully, remembering that your purpose is to help the writer do his or her best work. Keep in mind that an editor should always make positive, helpful comments that point to specific parts of the essay. After you have read the work, use the following questions to help you direct your comments:

☆ What did I like most about the biographical sketch?

☆ Can I see the person or event in my mind?

☆ Do I feel that I know the subject?

☆ Has the writer used details to describe the subject?

☆ What did the writer learn about his or her subject?

☆ What would I like to know more about?

PROOFREADING

When you are satisfied that your work says what you want it to say, check it carefully for errors in spelling, punctuation, grammar, and capitalization. Then make a neat, final copy of your biographical sketch.

PUBLISHING

After you revise your writing, you are ready to publish or share it. Put together a classroom portrait gallery called Someone You Should Know, and display the sketches for your classmates to read.

ASIAN AMERICANS IN PERFORMING ARTS

Have you ever thought about becoming a classical musician? An actor? A skater? Performing in front of an audience takes a special courage and special talents. In this unit, you will discover some of the ways the Asian Americans you will meet used their courage and talents to succeed in difficult and uncertain careers.

Vietnamese American actor **Dustin Nguyen** (NOO-yehn) says, "When I was growing up, I was desperately searching for a role model. There are a lot of problems trying to adapt to a new culture. If I can exert a certain amount of positive influence, then I am very happy with that."

Performing on stage seems natural to violinist **Midori** (mee-DOHR-ee), a Japanese American. "I feel so comfortable on stage; I feel safest. The best part of giving concerts is just being out there and playing, nothing else."

A talented ice skater of Japanese descent, **Kristi Yamaguchi** (yah–mah–GOO-chee) knew at the age of four that she wanted to be a skater. "There was never a point where I wanted to quit. Skating didn't come naturally, but I didn't mind working a little harder."

Haing Ngor (HAYN NOHR) has traveled many roads. "I have been many things in life. . . . But nothing has shaped my life as much as surviving the Pol Pot regime." [Pol Pot was the Communist dictator of Cambodia from 1975 to 1979.]

Korean American musician and conductor **Myung-Whun Chung** (MUNG-HUN CHUNG) was from a family that loved all kinds of music. In the words of his sister Myung-Wha, "It's not a matter of Western or Korean music. It's just music, inborn, ready to speak. It just needs to be brought out."

As you read this unit, think about the strength of each of these performers in the face of very demanding, and sometimes dangerous, situations.

DUSTIN NGUYEN

Dustin Nguyen, Vietnamese American actor, overcame his shyness by enrolling in an acting class. Nguyen believes it is his responsibility to be a positive role model for teenagers.

When people hear the words *Dustin* and *actor* in the same sentence, chances are they think of Academy Award-winning actor Dustin Hoffman. Some people, though, will think of another actor named Dustin—Vietnamese American actor Dustin Nguyen (NOO-yehn). How he found a new home and built a successful acting career is a story of overcoming obstacles.

Born on September 17, 1962, Dustin was given the Vietnamese name Nguyen Xuan Tri (NOO-yehn WAWN TREE). He and his mother, father, and younger brother lived very comfortably in Saigon (seye-GAHN), the capital of what was then South Vietnam. His mother was an actress and a dancer. His father was a television producer, director, and actor. They, like many other educated Vietnamese, spoke French and raised their children to appreciate French language and culture. As Dustin recalls, "From ages one to five, I went to a French kindergarten, so I spoke French probably better than I spoke Vietnamese." (See **Did You Know?** on page 123 for more information regarding the French influence in Vietnam.)

As Dustin was growing up, Vietnam was experiencing a great deal of unrest. During the 1950s, the Communists took control of the northern part of the country. Beginning in the early 1960s, they threatened to invade the south. Peace-keeping forces from the United Nations, as well as troops from France and the United States, became involved in the ongoing war. By the 1970s, the conflict had become a major cause of concern around the world. In the United States, it led to bitter arguments between those who thought it was morally wrong to be involved in the Vietnamese civil war and others who thought it was the duty of the United States to fight communism anywhere in the world.

During these times of conflict, the Nguyen family tried to lead a normal life. Eventually, however, they felt that they must speak out about the destruction of their country. Dustin's father began writing articles and TV scripts against the leaders of North Vietnam. "In his free time," Dustin explains, "my father wrote propaganda[1] . . . encouraging the North Vietnamese to defect"[2] and join the South Vietnamese. Taking such a stand was extremely dangerous. So, when the North Vietnamese invaded Saigon in 1975, Dustin's family had to flee.

The family hurried to the beach where a U.S. cargo ship was waiting to evacuate[3] hundreds of people. They took only the few possessions that they could carry. In the confusion, 12-year-old Dustin was separated from his family, but he caught up with his best friend. The two headed toward the water just as North Vietnamese soldiers opened fire. During those terrifying moments, Dustin's friend was shot. As he looked on helplessly, his friend died. In anguish,[4] Dustin ran with the crowd into the water and swam out to the ship. A few hours later, he found his parents and brother on board. Dustin was "safe," but he could not stop thinking about his friend's death.

Arriving in the United States, Dustin's family spent some time in a refugee camp[5] in Arkansas. Then the family moved to Kirkwood, Missouri. Dustin's parents took whatever jobs they could find. Many people helped them out, and eventually they moved into their own small house.

Everyone in the family took English lessons, but the language did not come easily at first. Indeed, the adjustment to a new life and a new culture was difficult for the Nguyens. No other Vietnamese people lived in the area. Also, the family felt that some

---

1. **propaganda** (prahp-uh-GAN-duh) *n.* ideas that are intended to influence people's opinions
2. **defect** (dee-FEKT) *v.* to leave one's country and join with another country that is opposed to the first one
3. **evacuate** (ee-VAK-yoo-ayt) *v.* to remove
4. **anguish** (ANG-gwihsh) *n.* great suffering and agony
5. **refugee camp** (rehf-yoo-GEE KAMP) a temporary living place set up for people who flee their home country for the safety of another country

people resented them. "The war was still fresh in people's minds," Dustin remembers. Some U.S. families had lost loved ones in the Vietnam War. "So there was a lot of hostility[6] toward us."

Unable to speak English well and shy by nature, Dustin found it hard to make friends. He realized that the key was learning English. "I made a real effort to learn the language. . . . English is the one thing that [made] it a lot easier. . . . The ability to communicate is so important. . . . You want to be able to have friends, and to be accepted."

Communicating and getting along with others became very important to Dustin. He improved his English, but he still lacked self-confidence. As a teenager, Dustin often felt lonely and unhappy. He needed to feel that he was good at something, so he decided to take a class in martial arts. He studied tae kwon do (TEYE KWUN DOH), and, at 17, he earned his second-degree black belt and won a Midwestern championship. "Martial arts became a very big part of my life," Dustin says. "I was not good at any other sports, and that had been difficult. To be able to compete was prestigious[7] and provided me with a sense of self-confidence and accomplishment. From there, I knew that I could be successful in other things in life."

Dustin's parents thought engineering would be a good field for him, so after he graduated from high school, he enrolled in Orange Coast College in Costa Mesa, California. But then something unexpected made Dustin realize that engineering was not for him. He took an acting class. "I was not really planning on becoming an actor, but I enrolled in an acting class because I was really shy," he says. "Once I started studying acting, I was fascinated by it." He decided to drop out of college to pursue an acting career.

At first, Dustin didn't tell his parents. When he finally did tell them that he had dropped out of college to become an actor,

6. **hostility** (hahs-TIHL-uh-tee) *n.* unfriendly actions
7. **prestigious** (prehs-TIHJ-uhs) *adj.* powerful because of wealth or fame

they were "very angry and disappointed." Dustin understood their disappointment. "They had worked very hard to put me through school. They felt I'd really let them down. It was the first time in my life that I did something against my parents' wishes." Yet, Dustin felt he needed to decide for himself what he wanted to do. "I wanted to do it so badly, and I knew I could be successful," he remembers.

It was a struggle at first—angering his parents, starting a new career, trying to figure out who he was. In 1981, he marked this turning point in his life by legally changing his name to Dustin Nguyen. Then he became a U.S. citizen, and headed for Hollywood. There, he took more acting classes and auditioned[8] for every part he could. His diligence[9] paid off. Dustin landed a role on an episode of the successful TV series *Magnum, P.I.* with Tom Selleck. Shortly after that, he worked on the daytime series *General Hospital* for almost a year.

A big break came in 1986. Dustin had auditioned for a part in a new TV series called *21 Jump Street.* Much to his delight, but not surprise, he got the job. By now, Dustin knew he had talent as an actor. The series lasted four seasons—a good run by TV standards. His success came quickly, but he knew there would always be risks. "I had to be willing to lose everything. Acting is such an insecure[10] and illogical profession," Dustin admitted later.

Nguyen's parents are now proud and supportive of him, and he realizes that their adjustment to a new life was as difficult as his was. For young people, he says, "having to adapt, learning a new language, and being able to retain your heritage is very confusing. Often parents are not as eager to make the transition, and rightfully so." Keeping one's heritage alive is very important but can be challenging, Dustin admits. "It's a big cultural

---

   8. auditioned (aw-DIHSH-uhnd) *v.* performed or acted at a tryout

   9. diligence (DIHL-uh-juhns) *n.* constant effort

   10. insecure (ihn-sih-KYOOR) *adj.* undependable or unreliable

struggle. For most Asian American kids, there's a lot of pressure to live the old way, the way your parents would like you to live." You have to strike your own balance and trust in your own ability, Dustin learned. "All I have to go on is my belief in myself."

The actor has not forgotten how hard it was for him growing up. He is active in such groups as DARE (Drug Abuse Resistance Education) and in suicide prevention efforts, volunteering his time to work with police and with teenagers. Nguyen is especially concerned about gang activity. He does all he can to discourage young people from getting involved in gangs, including making speeches and talking to people individually. If kids have "no role model or authority figure," he says, they may join gangs "as a substitution for [a] family atmosphere."

"When I was growing up," Dustin says, "I was desperately searching for that role model. There are a lot of problems trying to adapt to a new culture. If I can exert a certain amount of positive influence, then I am very happy with that."

Did You Know? *France colonized Vietnam during the 1800s, controlling the country's government and schools from 1883 to 1954. The French language and culture, therefore, have been evident in Vietnam since the 1800s. Even after Vietnam was freed from French rule in 1954, though, French influence remained, especially in the cities. Today, visitors to Ho Chi Minh (HOH CHEE MIHN) City (formerly Saigon), in what is now the Socialist Republic of Vietnam, can still dine in fine French restaurants, walk down streets with French names, and hear the French language spoken—all within the country of Vietnam.*

AFTER YOU READ

EXPLORING YOUR RESPONSES

1. When Dustin was forced to flee Saigon with his family, they could take little with them. Why do you think it is sometimes difficult to lose personal possessions?

2. Dustin got separated from his family as they waited to leave Saigon. How might you have felt in his place?

3. Imagine that you have just emigrated to another country. What is the first thing you will do? Why?

4. Dustin admitted that he was shy. How would you advise a person to overcome or understand shyness?

5. Dustin's parents wanted him to choose engineering because they viewed it as a secure career. How important do you think security is in choosing a career? Explain.

UNDERSTANDING WORDS IN CONTEXT

Read the following sentences from the biography. Think about what each underlined word means. In your notebook, write what the word means as it is used in the sentence.

1. Dustin explains, "My father wrote [articles] . . . encouraging the North Vietnamese to defect" and join the South Vietnamese.

2. The family hurried to the beach where a U.S. cargo ship was waiting to evacuate hundreds of people.

3. Dustin's friend was shot. As he looked on helplessly, his friend died. In anguish, Dustin ran with the crowd into the water and swam out to the ship.

4. Also, the family felt that some people resented them. . . . "There was a lot of hostility toward us."

5. There, he took more acting classes and [tried to win] every part he could. His <u>diligence</u> paid off. Dustin landed a role on an episode of the successful TV series *Magnum, P.I.*

RECALLING DETAILS

1. Describe the conflict in Vietnam in the 1970s.

2. Why did the Nguyens flee Saigon?

3. What happened on the beach as they prepared to leave?

4. How did studying tae kwon do help Dustin?

5. Why did Dustin take a class in acting?

UNDERSTANDING INFERENCES

In your notebook, write two or three sentences from the biography that support each of the following inferences.

1. Nguyen's parents loved their native country.

2. It was dangerous for people in Saigon to speak out against the Communists.

3. Dustin has had to cope with great changes.

4. The teenage years were especially challenging for Dustin.

5. Dustin learned that believing in oneself is the beginning of success.

INTERPRETING WHAT YOU HAVE READ

1. How do you think the Nguyen family's life was different in Saigon and the United States?

2. Besides grief over the loss of loved ones in the Vietnam War, what might have caused people in the United States to resent Vietnamese Americans?

3. Why do you think Dustin's parents, who had both been actors, wanted him to be an engineer?

4. How might an acting class have helped Dustin with his shyness?

5. Nguyen says, "Having to adapt [to a new culture] and being able to retain your heritage is very confusing." What do you think he means?

ANALYZING QUOTATIONS

Read the following quotation from the biography and answer the questions below.

> *"They had worked very hard to put me through school. They felt I'd really let them down. It was the first time in my life that I did something against my parents' wishes."*

1. What does the quote tell you about Nguyen's relationship with his parents?

2. In what ways did Nguyen think he let his parents down?

3. When do you think a person is right to make a choice that is different from the one his or her parents think is right? Give reasons for your opinion.

THINKING CRITICALLY

1. Dustin was a good student and can speak several languages. How might his academic and communication skills have helped him adjust to his new life?

2. Why do you think Nguyen changed his name?

3. Why do you think Dustin became involved in educating students about drugs and gangs?

4. Dustin says, "To be able to compete was prestigious." How do you think a person can gain prestige from competing?

5. Why do you think acting is considered to be a risky profession?

MIDORI

Midori, Japanese American violinist, began to play the violin at the age of 3. She is now an internationally known performer.

It was a warm, humid July evening at Tanglewood, a music festival, in the Berkshire Mountains of Massachusetts. A quiet 14-year-old, violin in hand, took her place on stage with the Boston Symphony Orchestra. Leading the orchestra was the well-known conductor Leonard Bernstein. It was one of his compositions, *Serenade*, that the orchestra was about to perform. He raised his baton, and the concert began.

Suddenly, the E string on the young violinist's instrument snapped. She calmly approached the concertmaster, and, as is the custom, borrowed his violin. She played smoothly until, all at once, the E string broke on *this* instrument. Still unflustered, she borrowed the associate concertmaster's violin and finished the *Serenade* in triumph.

Bernstein, the orchestra, and the audience burst into a "cheering, stomping, whistling ovation,"[1] according to reporters. The front page of the *New York Times* read, "Girl, 14, Conquers Tanglewood with 3 Violins." Next to the headline was a photo of the brilliant, confident violinist, Midori (mee-DOHR-ee).

Midori Goto (GOH-toh), who performs under the name Midori, has proven to be much more than just a child prodigy.[2] She has become an internationally known violin virtuoso,[3] a musician of great technical and artistic skill.

Born in Osaka, Japan, in 1971, Midori showed an aptitude[4] for music at an early age. Her mother, a teacher and professional violinist, took the toddler with her to rehearsals. Little Midori

---

1. **ovation** (oh-VAY-shuhn) *n.* enthusiastic applause
2. **prodigy** (PRAHD-uh-jee) *n.* an unusually talented person
3. **virtuoso** (ver-choo-OH-soh) *n.* a person performing with great skill
4. **aptitude** (AP-tuh-tood) *n.* a natural ability or talent

would listen attentively, her mother recalls. "She often slept by the front row of the auditorium when I rehearsed. One day I heard her humming a Bach concerto—the very piece I'd been practicing two days before." On Midori's third birthday, her mother gave her a real violin. It was one-sixteenth the size of an adult violin. But she made a big sound with it.

For Midori, learning to play the violin was almost as natural as learning to talk. Her mother was her first teacher, yet, according to Midori, "[She] didn't force me to play the violin. She only taught me because I wanted to learn." Midori practiced and memorized countless well-known classical pieces of music, often in an empty room down the hall from where her mother's orchestra rehearsed. When she was 6 years old, Midori gave her first recital in public.

Soon Midori's talent was gaining attention. When she was 8 years old, a friend of her mother's from the United States happened to hear Midori play. She knew Midori was special and quickly sent a tape recording to the Juilliard (JOO-lee-ahrd) School of Music in New York City. The instructor who listened to the tape, Dorothy DeLay, found the music to be "absolutely extraordinary." She invited Midori to attend the Aspen Summer Music Festival in Colorado in 1981. DeLay even arranged a scholarship for her.

Midori made quite a splash at the festival. Pinchas Zukerman (PEEN-kuhs ZOOK-uhr-mahn), a famous violinist and conductor, recalls her performance: "Out comes this tiny little thing, not even 10 at the time. . . . She tuned [her violin], she bowed to the audience, she bowed to me, she bowed to the pianist—and then she played the Bartok concerto, and I went bananas. . . . She had a tiny little half-size violin, but the sound that came out. . . . I was absolutely stunned."

One year later, Midori and her mother moved to New York City. Midori enrolled in the precollege division of Juilliard on a full scholarship. It was a tough time for her. Not only was she adjusting to a new language and culture, but also her parents' "arranged" marriage was ending in divorce. (See **Did You**

Know? on page 132 for more information on arranged marriages.) So, Midori and her mother were starting a new life together in a strange land. Always close, the relationship between mother and daughter was now even stronger.

But Midori adjusted. She managed to get through her schoolwork during the week, practice the violin for hours every day, and take music lessons on Saturdays. She also occasionally performed with the New York Philharmonic Orchestra for Young People. Midori admits, "It was very difficult. It was the first time I went to a music school, the first time I had a teacher. Also I had never been around so many kids before!" To support the two of them, Midori's mother took a job teaching violin.

Recalling this time, Midori appreciates her mother's strength. Mrs. Goto had left Japan with a small child, which greatly worried her relatives. Had she made the right decision? Would they ever see her again? Midori remembers, "When she decided to bring me here [to New York] . . . we had no money and could not even speak English. . . . It took amazing conviction[5] to come alone to a foreign country with a little kid, and to go against the family wishes. I like to think I have some of that strong-mindedness."

Indeed, she does. This streak of strong-mindedness first came to the surface in 1987, when Midori decided to leave Juilliard. Her mother, her teachers, and her agent—the person who handles her business arrangements—all disapproved. They felt that, at 15, Midori was still too young to make such an important decision. But she was firm—and perhaps a little rebellious. As Midori explains, "Between school homework, rehearsals, and practice there was no time for anything else. Since dropping out of Juilliard, the world has opened. I go to concerts and movies and have a special curiosity to hear how this one plays and that one plays. I love it."

---

5. **conviction** (kuhn-VIHK-shuhn) *n.* strong belief

So, in 1987, Midori began her life as a full-time violinist. She continued her academic studies, but her focus was now on preparing for her professional debut.[6] This public recital would show people whether or not she was serious about music. It would also show whether she could play well, not just for a child, but for an adult. To help prepare her, Midori's agent scheduled dozens of "training" concerts for small audiences. For the next three years, Midori traveled, practiced, performed—and still did several hours of homework every day.

Carnegie Hall in New York City is one of the most famous concert stages in the world. Though Midori had played there with an orchestra once before, she had never walked on the stage under the spotlights all alone. In this great hall, Midori would make her debut as a solo performer. In the fall of 1990, she was ready.

Carnegie Hall was sold out that night. A recording company had several cameras and microphones in place to tape the performance for laser disk and home video. As she came on stage, Midori was poised[7] and confident. If she was nervous, it did not show. Weeks earlier she had said, "I feel so comfortable on stage; I feel safest. The best part of giving concerts is just being out there and playing, nothing else."

Midori played many long, difficult classical pieces that night. Each piece made special demands on her as an artist, and as a person. She had to express the full range of emotions—happiness and sadness, anger and tenderness. Her performance was breathtaking. Critics described it as "absolutely unique" and "strikingly mature." The audience was transfixed.[8] The evening ended with a standing ovation. The applause was deafening.

Midori's flawless recital helped launch her into a successful career. The years of practice were paying off, but life did not

---

6. **debut** (day-BYOO) *n.* the first formal appearance
7. **poised** (POIZD) *adj.* calm; ready
8. **transfixed** (tranz-FIHKST) *adj.* made motionless

become instantly easy—and certainly not "glamorous." Not yet 20, Midori was juggling her sudden fame, financial success, and world concert tours. The public would be watching to see how she handled all this—the celebrity[9] *and* the responsibility.

Midori seems to be managing quite well—both in her personal and her professional life. She loves to read, and she enjoys writing short stories. In fact, she is a regular contributor to a Japanese magazine for teens. Midori also studies karate, goes to concerts, and shops for books and CDs in her free time. Her favorite hobby, though, is cooking. This might surprise anyone who knows Midori, who is a light eater. "That's the only time my mom forces me to do anything: she tells me to eat," Midori laughs.

Midori performs about 80 concerts a year, appearing with many of the world's best orchestras and most famous conductors. She also has a contract with a major recording company. How does Midori feel about the pressure, the praise—and, sometimes, the criticism? She seems to take it all in stride. In fact, she is probably her own biggest critic: "After a concert I rate my performance. What was good? What was not so good? Then I tell myself that I'm not a robot." While robots may make fewer mistakes than humans do, they do not play the violin the way Midori does.

Did You Know? *Following the traditional Japanese custom, Midori's mother and father had an arranged marriage. In an arranged marriage, parents decide when their children are very young whom they will marry when they grow up. The couple's feelings are not taken into account. Often, arranged marriages have a political or a financial purpose. Some turn out very well; others do not. The custom is dying in Japan, as Western ideas of freedom of choice and romance are becoming accepted by younger Japanese.*

---

9. celebrity (suh-LEHB-ruh-tee) *n.* wide recognition; fame

AFTER YOU READ

EXPLORING YOUR RESPONSES

1. For Midori, learning to play the violin was as natural as learning to talk. Describe some things you have seen some small children do that many adults would not be able to accomplish.

2. Midori and her mother left Japan so that Midori could develop her musical talent. How might such a move affect a person's life?

3. Midori's mother and others disapproved of Midori's decision to leave Juilliard. What might you have advised her to do? Explain.

4. What do you think are the pros and cons of becoming successful at a very young age?

5. Midori doesn't feel nervous performing for large audiences. When you feel nervous, what do you do?

UNDERSTANDING WORDS IN CONTEXT

Read the following sentences from the biography. Think about what each underlined word means. In your notebook, write what the word means as it is used in the sentence.

1. Midori Goto, who performs under the name Midori, has proven to be much more than just a child prodigy. She has become an internationally known violin virtuoso.

2. "We had no money and could not even speak English. . . . It took amazing conviction to come alone to a foreign country with a little kid, and to go against the family wishes."

3. Midori showed an aptitude for music at an early age. Her mother, a teacher and professional violinist, took the toddler with her to rehearsals. Little Midori would listen attentively.

4. She continued her academic studies, but her focus was now on preparing for her professional <u>debut</u>. This public recital would show people whether or not she was serious about music.

5. Her performance was breathtaking. . . . The audience was <u>transfixed</u>. The evening ended with a standing ovation.

RECALLING DETAILS

1. When did Midori's interest in music become obvious?
2. Who taught Midori how to play the violin?
3. Why did Midori and her mother come to the United States?
4. How did Midori respond to breaking a violin string at the Tanglewood concert?
5. Why did Midori leave Juilliard?

UNDERSTANDING INFERENCES

In your notebook, write two or three sentences from the biography that support each of the following inferences.

1. Midori's mother has a great influence on her.
2. It is unusual for a 14-year-old to perform classical music.
3. The young musician sacrificed some things to pursue what she wanted.
4. Being a professional musician requires more than talent.
5. Midori has tried to develop other skills and interests.

INTERPRETING WHAT YOU HAVE READ

1. At the Tanglewood concert, Midori remained calm when her violin string broke—twice. What does this tell you about her?
2. Midori said her mother showed "amazing conviction to come alone to a foreign country with a little kid and to go against the family wishes." What does this quote tell you about Midori's family?

3. What might Midori's life have been like if she had stayed at Juilliard?

4. What things might have contributed to the close relationship between Midori and her mother?

5. Why might Midori be better able to handle "instant" fame than some people?

ANALYZING QUOTATIONS

Read the following quotation from the biography. Then answer the questions.

> *"It was very difficult. It was the first time I went to a music school, the first time I had a teacher. Also I had never been around so many kids before!"*

1. Why do you think it was difficult for Midori to adjust to having a music teacher in a music school?

2. Based on this quote, describe what you think Midori's young life was like.

3. What kinds of things does a person have to adjust to in a new school?

THINKING CRITICALLY

1. Do you think Midori *chose* to be a violinist? Explain.

2. How might Midori's life have been different if she and her mother had stayed in Japan?

3. How might Midori's career have been different if she began performing when she was older?

4. How do you think Midori's life is different from and similar to that of most young women in the United States today?

5. What are some advantages and disadvantages of performing at a young age?

Kristi Yamaguchi, Japanese American figure skater, displays her artistry on the ice. Yamaguchi dreamed of winning the Olympic gold medal, and in 1992, she achieved that dream.

There is some truth to the expression, "The early bird catches the worm," at least as far as Kristi Yamaguchi (yah-mah-GOO-chee) is concerned. When most people her age were asleep, Kristi was out on the ice practicing to make a dream come true.

Starting when Kristi was in fourth grade, her mother, Carole, woke Kristi at 4:00 A.M. Before the sun came up, they drove to the ice skating rink. There Kristi practiced skating with her coach, Christy Kjarsgaard (CHAHRS-gahrd), for the next five hours. By the time many people are just settling down to work, Kristi had already put in a full day.

Kristi Yamaguchi, who was born in 1971 in Hayward, California, had dreamed of being a famous ice skater since she was 4 years old. That was when she saw her first ice show. She loved the skaters' colorful costumes and admired the graceful shapes, or figures, their skates traced on the ice. What she saw was magical—leaps and speeds that were dizzying to watch.

That same year, 1976, Kristi watched on television as U.S. skater Dorothy Hamill won the gold medal in the women's figure skating event at the Winter Olympic Games. Hamill's win made her the most famous woman figure skater in the world. It also helped Kristi Yamaguchi make up her mind. Like Hamill, she would be a skater and go to the Olympics someday.

Kristi asked her parents for skating lessons, but they said she would have to wait until she was 6 years old. So Kristi waited, carrying her Dorothy Hamill doll. Two years later she reminded her parents of their promise. Seeing that Kristi was serious, the Yamaguchis kept their word.

Fortunately, the Yamaguchis could afford lessons for their three athletic children, Lori, Kristi, and Brett. Jim was a dentist, and Carole was a doctor's secretary. They were not rich, but they lived a comfortable life in Fremont, California, near San Francisco. Few people realize the cost of training a competitive[1] athlete. Jim Yamaguchi once said that Kristi's skating lessons cost as much each year as going to a top college.

Kristi's parents can remember less comfortable times in their own childhood. They had both spent time in internment camps during World War II. (See **Did You Know?**, on page 141, and the biography of Yoshiko Uchida, on pages 42-48, for more information on internment camps.) Carole, in fact, had been born in a camp in Colorado. Like many Japanese Americans, Carole's and Jim's families lost all they owned. Also like many Japanese Americans, Carole and Jim still find it hard to discuss the camps. While making their children aware of the past, the couple has chosen to focus on the future. The Yamaguchis' three children have helped to brighten that future considerably.

Kristi Yamaguchi was not a good skater at first. Still, she knew she was doing the right thing. "The first time I put on the skates, I just loved it," she remembers. "There was never a point where I wanted to quit. Skating didn't come naturally, but I didn't mind working a little harder." Why did she love skating? "There's a sense of freedom. You feel the wind flowing, and you're gliding across the ice. It's fun."

Kristi entered her first skating contest when she was 8 years old. After that, she spent most of her time skating—and winning prizes. Somehow she got through her schoolwork, and she even found time for a little social life. "Once I'm away from the rink, I'm a normal person," she insists. Admitting that she did have to miss some fun times because of her skating, Kristi nevertheless says, "I gained so much in skating. I wouldn't trade it for anything."

In her senior year in high school, Yamaguchi had a hard decision to make. Christy Kjarsgaard, her coach and close friend, had just married and moved to Edmonton, Alberta. If Kristi wanted to go on training with Kjarsgaard, she would have to move to Canada.

Yamaguchi's drive to learn more was strong. She moved to Edmonton the day after she graduated from high school. Her

---

1. **competitive** (kuhm-PEHT-uh-tihv) *adj.* trying to win a contest

coach thinks the move helped Kristi grow up, both as a person and as a skater. "Kristi has gone from this little kid to a young woman," Kjarsgaard-Ness said after the move. ". . . That comes through on the ice."

Yamaguchi's career took off when she won the world women's figure skating championship in 1991. A victory at the U.S. national championship in January 1992 followed. In that same month she qualified[2] to enter the biggest contest of all–the 1992 Winter Olympics in Albertville, France.

Athletes from all over the world compete in the Olympics. Yet, of the 29 women in the figure skating event, the two most likely winners had Japanese surnames.[3] One was Kristi Yamaguchi, a fourth-generation Japanese American. The other was Midori Ito (mih-DOHR-ee EE-toh) of Nagoya, Japan.

The two young women, Yamaguchi, 20 years old, and Ito, 22, had very different skating styles. Midori Ito was a jumper. In 1988 she became the first woman to do a very difficult jump, the triple Axel (named after Axel Paulsen, a Norwegian ice skater). The jump involves spinning in the air three-and-a-half times–not just three times as in other triple jumps. If Ito completed a triple Axel in her Olympic performance, the judges were sure to give her high scores.

Kristi Yamaguchi had never successfully completed a triple Axel, and her Olympic programs did not include one. But they did include other triple jumps, some of which are almost as hard as the triple Axel is. More importantly, Yamaguchi had something that many people felt the shorter, more powerful Ito did not have–grace and artistry[4] on the ice. Kristi was as much a dancer as she was an athlete.

The first part of the women's figure skating event is called the short program. In this part, each skater performs to music for 2 minutes and 40 seconds. All skaters are required to include

2. **qualified** (KWAHL-ih-feyed) *v.* met requirements

3. **surnames** (SER-naymz) *n. pl.* family names or last names

4. **artistry** (AHRT-ihs-tree) *n.* artistic ability or work

certain elements[5] in their programs. However, each skater decides when and how to include them, which is why the programs look so different.

On Wednesday evening, February 19, 1992, Midori Ito was greeted with loud cheers as she skated onto the ice. Ito had planned to include a triple Axel in her short program. At the last minute, however, Midori and her coach decided on a more conservative[6] approach. Instead of the Axel, she tried an easier triple jump. To everyone's amazement, Ito fell, even though she had always done the jump well before. As a result, Ito won only fourth place in the short program.

Kristi Yamaguchi's short program, by contrast, was nearly perfect. As one reporter wrote, she "fairly floated from one required element of her program to the next." The nine judges gave Kristi the highest scores of all the skaters.

Yamaguchi knew that this victory did not mean that the gold medal was hers. One of the other skaters might give a better performance than she did in the long program, the second part of the contest. Ito's famous triple Axel, for example, might give her the victory.

In the long program, each contestant skates to music for four minutes. Skaters are free to choose all their own movements and jumps. Kristi and the others would be judged on both their technical[7] skill and their artistry. In addition to the Olympic judges, millions of people all over the world would be watching them.

Midori Ito tried a triple Axel early in her program, but she fell. Most skaters would not have attempted another hard jump after falling. Ito had courage, however. She tried the Axel once again toward the end of her program—and this time, she made it! She became the first woman to do a triple Axel in the Olympics.

---

5. **elements** (EHL-uh-muhnts) *n. pl.* parts; specific patterns or movements

6. **conservative** (kuhn-SER-vuh-tihv) *adj.* cautious; safe

7. **technical** (TEHK-nih-kuhl) *adj.* showing the practical skills of science or art

Kristi Yamaguchi began her long program with two difficult triple jumps—but not Axels. Her jumps were perfect, just like almost everything else about her performance. Only once in her program, in fact, did she falter. While doing a triple jump that usually was easy for her, Kristi started to fall. But she caught herself with a graceful touch of her hand on the ice.

The judges again gave Yamaguchi the highest scores of all the competitors. Although she did not receive the perfect score of "6" from any of the judges, eight of nine did give her "5.9" for "artistic impression." A reporter wrote, "They loved Yamaguchi's grace. . . . They loved her speed, her consistency[8] under pressure, the variety of skills displayed within her program. And, yes, they loved her artistry. . . . Yamaguchi, [even] without the triple Axel, is as close to a complete package as women's skating ever has seen." Midori Ito's courage and spectacular jump won her the silver medal—second prize.

Kristi Yamaguchi was thrilled to win the gold medal. "It's something I've dreamed of ever since I put on skates as a little girl," she told reporters afterward. Perhaps she remembered herself at 5 years old, clutching her Dorothy Hamill doll and dreaming of the medal she would earn for the United States, and for herself.

> **Did You Know?** *An order signed on February 19, 1942, by President Franklin D. Roosevelt established "internment camps," in which Japanese Americans were imprisoned until the end of World War II. Most of the Japanese Americans in the western United States were taken from their homes, stripped of most of their possessions, and forced to live in cramped, uncomfortable conditions simply because of their cultural background.*
>
> *It was not until 1983 that a government study concluded that "a grave injustice was done to Japanese Americans." The causes of the uprooting were prejudice*

---

8. **consistency** (kuhn-SIHS-tuhn-see) *n.* agreement with what has already been done or expressed

and poor judgment caused in part by the unusual circumstances of war. In 1990 the U.S. Congress passed Public Law 101-162, which was an attempt to make up for the suffering of the internees, or Japanese Americans who had been sent to internment camps. Each of the 60,000 survivors was given $20,000.

EXPLORING YOUR RESPONSES

1. Kristi Yamaguchi first thought about skating when she saw Dorothy Hamill win the gold medal. How important are role models like Hamill in helping people achieve their goals?

2. Yamaguchi began skating lessons when she was 6 years old. Do you think someone could become an Olympic gold medalist if he or she started skating as a teen-ager? Explain.

3. Yamaguchi trained with a talented coach named Christy Kjarsgaard-Ness. If you could chose anyone in the world to teach you something, who would that person be? Explain.

4. A combination of dreaming and working hard helped Yamaguchi win the gold medal. How do these two actions work together to help a person achieve a goal?

5. Yamaguchi is very happy with her Olympic success. Do you think it is possible to be happy even if you do not achieve your highest goals? Why or why not?

UNDERSTANDING WORDS IN CONTEXT

Read the following sentences from the biography. Think about what each underlined word means. In your notebook, write what the word means as it is used in the sentence.

1. In that same month, she <u>qualified</u> to enter the biggest contest of all—the 1992 Winter Olympics in Albertville, France.

2. The two most likely winners had Japanese <u>surnames</u>. One was Kristi Yamaguchi, a fourth-generation Japanese American.

3. At the last minute, however, Midori and her coach decided on a more <u>conservative</u> approach. Instead of the Axel, she tried an easier triple jump.

4. Yamaguchi had something that many people felt the shorter, more powerful Ito did not have–grace and <u>artistry</u> on the ice. Kristi was as much a dancer as she was an athlete.

5. A reporter wrote, "They loved Yamaguchi's grace. . . . They loved her speed, her <u>consistency</u> under pressure, the variety of skills displayed within her program."

RECALLING DETAILS

1. How did Kristi become interested in figure skating?

2. How was Kristi's life different from that of other people her age?

3. What happened to Kristi's parents during World War II?

4. Why did Kristi move to Canada?

5. Why was Yamaguchi worried about competing against Ito?

UNDERSTANDING INFERENCES

In your notebook, write two or three sentences from the biography that support each of the following inferences.

1. Kristi Yamaguchi enjoys skating.

2. Yamaguchi is willing to give up things to achieve a goal.

3. Yamaguchi and Ito both have a strong drive to win.

4. Yamaguchi's success was achieved with the help of others.

5. Strategy plays a part in success.

INTERPRETING WHAT YOU HAVE READ

1. Kristi asked her parents for skating lessons when she was 4 years old. Why do you think they made her wait until she was 6 to begin?

2. Yamaguchi says she has gained so much from skating that she "wouldn't trade it for anything." Besides prizes and medals, what do you think Yamaguchi has gained?

3. Why did Yamaguchi's move to Canada "help her grow up"?

4. Why do you think Yamaguchi decided not to do a triple Axel jump in her Olympic performance even though Midori Ito planned to do one?

5. Kristi wrote "Always dream" on pictures she autographed a few months before the Olympics. What did she mean?

ANALYZING QUOTATIONS

Read the following quotation from the biography and answer the questions below.

> "Skating didn't come naturally, but I didn't mind working a little harder."

1. What do you think Yamaguchi means when she says, "Skating didn't come naturally"?

2. What are the advantages and disadvantages of skills that "come naturally"?

3. How can family, friends, and school help a person discover what he or she does well?

THINKING CRITICALLY

1. Kristi Yamaguchi's parents supported her dream in many ways. Do you think she could have achieved her goal without their support? Explain.

2. How do you think Yamaguchi's skating was affected by her competition with Ito?

3. Besides talent and hard work, what other qualities do you think figure skaters need? Explain.

4. What do Olympic skating judges look for in evaluating an athlete's performance?

5. Kristi Yamaguchi's training prevented her from doing many things people her age usually do. Do you think any goal is worth this sacrifice? Explain.

HAING NGOR

Haing Ngor, Cambodian American doctor and actor, is shown here at the 1985 Academy Awards ceremony. Ngor won the Oscar for Best Supporting Actor for his role in the film *The Killing Fields*.

Here is how Haing Ngor (HAYN NOHR) sums up his remarkable life: "I have been many things in life. A trader walking barefoot on paths through the jungles. A medical doctor, driving to his clinic in a shiny Mercedes. In the past few years, to the surprise of many people, and above all myself, I have been a Hollywood actor. But nothing has shaped my life as much as surviving the Pol Pot regime.[1] I am a survivor of the Cambodian holocaust.[2] That's who I am."

During the late 1970s, more than one million Cambodians were killed or starved to death under Communist dictator[3] Pol Pot. By acting in a movie called *The Killing Fields*, Haing Ngor has helped educate the world about the terror of those years. (See **Did You Know?** on page 151 for more information on Pol Pot.)

Haing Ngor grew up in a small village south of Phnom Penh (PAH-nohm PEHN), the capital of Cambodia. His parents were wealthy, and it seemed they could provide their large family (five sons and three daughters) with a pleasant life. During Haing's childhood, however, Cambodia was torn apart by war. The Ngor family was not able to escape the chaos[4] that resulted.

Beginning in the 1940s, many Cambodians living in the countryside began to rebel against the French, who had controlled the country since 1863. Wealthy people like the Ngors were viewed as the enemy by many Cambodians. Haing's father was kidnapped several times and held for ransom.[5]

---

1. **regime** (ruh-ZHEEM) *n.* the time a particular leader is in power
2. **holocaust** (HAHL-uh-kawst) *n.* a great or total destruction of life
3. **dictator** (DIHK-tayt-uhr) *n.* a ruler with complete power
4. **chaos** (KAY-ahs) *n.* a state of total confusion
5. **ransom** (RAN-suhm) *n.* the payment of money or agreement to meet some other demand in exchange for a captive person's release

Perhaps in response to the unrest around him, Haing was tough and bold as a boy. "I had a short attention span and far too much energy. I liked sports. I loved fighting. My gang, from the western side of the village, was always getting in fights with the gang from the eastern side of the village." Later, this toughness would help save his life.

In 1953, under its leader Norodom Sihanouk (NUR-uh-duhm SEE-ah-nuhk), Cambodia won its independence from France. The country became peaceful for a time, and the Ngor family's trading company became successful again. Haing did well in school because he had a goal. He wanted to study medicine.

Ngor's father, however, wanted his son to join the family business. "What?" he asked angrily when Haing announced his plan. "Seven more years before you can make any money? You expect me to pay for you to study while the rest of us are working?" But Haing's mother eventually changed her husband's mind. The family even helped pay for Ngor's education.

Ngor liked the idea of being a doctor. People looked up to doctors, and doctors could live comfortably. But he also had a less selfish reason to study medicine. "There were many sick people in Cambodia. . . . Hygiene[6] was not good. . . . I saw children, old people, wounded people, many in rural villages, but no medicine. As a doctor, at least I could do something for my village."

Ngor specialized in gynecology (geye-nih-KAHL-uh-jee) and obstetrics (uhb-STEH-trihks), branches of medicine that deal with women's health and childbirth. While he was tutoring students to raise money for school expenses, Haing met a young woman named Chang My Huoy (CHAHNG MEE HOI), whom he later married.

Life was good for the young doctor. "In 1968, I got two Mercedes. I paid cash. One was for my girlfriend. I let her have her own car, and I had mine. I would say, 'Don't cook. We will go out to eat.'" But things would soon change.

---

6. **Hygiene** (HEYE-jeen) *n.* practices designed to keep people healthy and clean

By this time, the ongoing war in neighboring Vietnam had become fierce. (See the biography of Dustin Nguyen on page 119–123 for more information on the Vietnam war.) Sihanouk tried to keep Cambodia out of the war, but Vietnamese Communists used roads through Cambodia to send supplies to their troops. To stop this activity, U.S. forces began to bomb parts of Cambodia. Then, Sihanouk was overthrown in 1970 and replaced by the pro-U.S. General Lon Nol (LAWN NOHL). Meanwhile, Communist rebels called the Khmer Rouge (kuh-MEHR ROOJ) fought to overthrow the new Cambodian government. Khmer Rouge leader Pol Pot declared that he would build a new society based on farming and shared wealth. Anyone with money and an education, like Ngor, was the enemy.

On April 17, 1975, Haing discovered exactly how dangerous his position was. That day he was operating on a patient in the hospital in Phnom Penh. About 11 other staff members were in the operating room with him. Suddenly, Khmer Rouge soldiers burst in and held rifles to Ngor's head. "You the doctor?" they demanded. Ngor told them the doctor had just left. He might fool them for a moment, but that was all.

Ngor and his staff fled the hospital, leaving the patient on the operating table. Haing knew that the patient was dying. He also knew that he and his staff would be shot if they did not run. He chose to save 12 lives instead of one. The memory of that day will always haunt Ngor.

From that day on, Haing's life turned upside down. Pol Pot ordered people out of the cities. Millions poured into the countryside—without money or, for many, the know-how to survive. Haing Ngor and his wife were among them.

In the countryside, Haing and Huoy ate whatever they could find—snails, grasshoppers, mice, even leaves. All the time, Ngor had to keep his identity as a doctor secret. Nevertheless, the Khmer Rouge captured him three times, once cutting off a finger because, in Ngor's words, " . . . someone had told them I stole something to eat." Food was scarce and medical supplies were even harder to find. Huoy died in 1978, while pregnant with their child.

Finally, in 1979, invading Vietnamese troops drove the Khmer Rouge away. Ngor escaped to nearby Thailand. In 1980, Haing was able to get a seat on a plane to the United States that was packed with other refugees.

Ngor did not have a U.S. medical license, so he could not work as a doctor. Instead, he got a job with the Chinatown Service Center, which offered services to Vietnamese, Cambodian, and Laotian refugees. The fact that Ngor speaks nine languages, including English, made starting life over and helping other refugees much easier.

Meanwhile, the producers of the movie *The Killing Fields* were looking for an actor to play a Cambodian named Dith Pran (DIHTH PRAWN). Pran, a correspondent[7] for the *New York Times,* had suffered under the Khmer Rouge in many of the ways Ngor had. The film's casting director[8] saw Ngor at a wedding in Los Angeles, and she took several pictures of him. The director was impressed with what he saw and invited Ngor to try out for the part.

Although Ngor had no experience as a movie actor, to survive Pol Pot's dictatorship he had acted every day. He was Haing Ngor, taxi driver, not Haing Ngor, doctor. His acting ability had helped save his life. During the tryout, Ngor's handling of a very emotional scene was so skillful that he got the job on the spot. The director remembers, "I asked him [Ngor] to pretend to persuade Pat Golden, reading for Pran's wife, to leave the country. He cried, and he made Pat cry. He did it five times. At that point, I knew this was an actor."

For Ngor, creating the character of Dith Pran came naturally. He had 34 years of sorrows, regrets, fears, and hopes to draw on. He knew what it was like to build a life and have it destroyed. Ngor's performance was so convincing and powerful that he won the Academy Award Oscar in 1985 for Best Supporting Actor.

---

7. **correspondent** (kawr-uh-SPAHN-duhnt) *n.* a person who makes regular reports to a newspaper, magazine, or broadcast network

8. **casting director** the person who chooses the actors for parts in movies, TV programs, and plays

Haing Ngor continues to act occasionally in TV and movies. But he spends most of his time educating people about Cambodia under the Khmer Rouge. His autobiography, *A Cambodian Odyssey,*[9] both horrifies and fascinates readers. Ngor's next book, *The Healing Fields*, deals with the problems of refugees around the world. Much of the money Haing has earned from acting and writing he has contributed to refugee relief efforts.

His role as Dith Pran has helped Ngor deal with feelings of guilt and grief. By playing the part so well, he paid a tribute to his family and homeland–and to Pran himself, who has become a close friend. Ngor says of his performance, "My heart is satisfied. I have done something perfect."

> **Did You Know?** *In 1976, Pol Pot was named premier of Kampuchea (kam-poo-CHEE-uh), as Cambodia was called from 1975 to 1989. His regime is considered by many historians to be one of the cruelest in modern history. It controlled people with fear–fear of losing property, loved ones, or their own lives. The official estimate of the number of people who died under Pol Pot is one million, but some unofficial estimates report as many as three million deaths. Chinese Communists supported Pol Pot. This threatened Vietnamese Communists, who were backed by the USSR. In 1979, Vietnamese Communists invaded Cambodia, and Pol Pot fled to China. During the 1980s, the Vietnamese-backed Cambodian government and the exiled Khmer Rouge struggled for control. In 1991, the two groups signed a treaty and began to rule Cambodia together until elections could be held.*

9. **Odyssey** (AHD-ih-see) *n.* a long wandering or journey

AFTER YOU READ

EXPLORING YOUR RESPONSES

1. Haing has said that he had "a short attention span" and "too much energy" until he found a goal. What positive effects has setting a goal had on you or someone you know?

2. Ngor thought being a doctor would allow him to help people. What career or careers sound interesting to you? Explain.

3. Ngor did something creative to deal with his difficult past—he acted. How else can people deal with difficult situations?

4. Although Ngor came close to dying several times, he was able to survive. What qualities do you think a person needs in order to survive such dangerous situations? Explain.

5. Haing Ngor has helped millions of people learn about Cambodian life under the Communist dictator Pol Pot. Do you think it is important for people to know about the suffering of others? Explain.

UNDERSTANDING WORDS IN CONTEXT

Read the following sentences from the biography. Think about what each underlined word means. In your notebook, write what the word means as it is used in the sentence.

1. "I am a survivor of the Cambodian holocaust. . . ." During the late 1970s, more than one million Cambodians were killed or starved to death under Communist dictator Pol Pot.

2. Cambodia was torn apart by war. The Ngor family was not able to escape the chaos that resulted.

3. Wealthy people like the Ngors were viewed as the enemy by many Cambodians. Haing's father was kidnapped several times and held for ransom.

4. [Dith] Pran, a <u>correspondent</u> for the *New York Times*, had suffered under the Khmer Rouge in many of the ways Ngor had.

5. The film's <u>casting director</u> saw Ngor at a wedding in Los Angeles, and she took several pictures of him. The director was impressed . . . and invited Ngor to try out for the part.

RECALLING DETAILS

1. In what movie did Haing Ngor act?

2. Why was his father originally upset with Haing's choice of career?

3. Why did Ngor say he was not a doctor?

4. How was Ngor's life different before and after the Khmer Rouge came to power?

5. What skills helped Haing Ngor adjust to life in the United States?

UNDERSTANDING INFERENCES

In your notebook, write two or three sentences from the biography that support each of the following inferences.

1. Haing Ngor has found ways to deal with his feelings about the Khmer Rouge.

2. Life under Pol Pot was deadly for many Cambodians.

3. Ngor is able to adapt to changing situations.

4. Sometimes people do things they never expected to do.

5. Personal experiences can sometimes help an actor as much as acting experience can.

INTERPRETING WHAT YOU HAVE READ

1. Describe the society the Khmer Rouge wanted to establish.

2. What effect did Pol Pot's government have on Ngor and other professionals?

3. Why do you think Haing Ngor feels guilty about his past?

4. What signs of independence did Haing show as a youth?

5. How did Ngor's experiences under Pol Pot and the Khmer Rouge help him win an Oscar for his performance in *The Killing Fields*?

ANALYZING QUOTATIONS

Read the following quotation from the biography and answer the questions below.

> *"Nothing has shaped my life as much as surviving the Pol Pot regime. I am a survivor of the Cambodian holocaust. That's who I am."*

1. Why do you think Ngor chose to describe himself in this way?

2. How can surviving something difficult help people grow and discover who they are?

3. Think of a phrase to describe yourself or someone you admire. Explain why you chose that phrase.

THINKING CRITICALLY

1. How do you think Ngor feels about war?

2. When Khmer Rouge soldiers invaded the operating room, Ngor left his patient and fled. Do you think it is possible to say Ngor was either right or wrong in doing this? Explain.

3. The Khmer Rouge wanted to create a society in which there were no rich or poor. What kind of society do you think would be best? Explain.

4. Why do you think Ngor wants to tell the world about the Cambodian holocaust rather than put the past behind him?

5. Ngor uses his skill and experience to help people learn about the past. What has his story taught you?

MYUNG-WHUN CHUNG

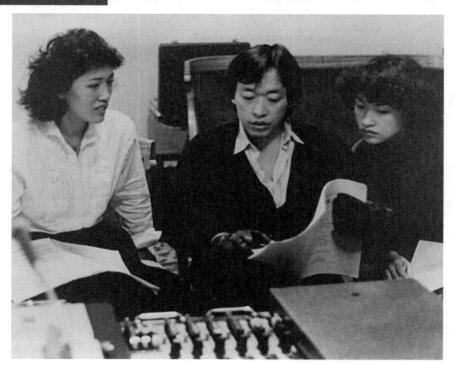

Myung-Whun Chung, Korean American pianist and conductor, discusses a piece of music with his sisters Myung-Wha Chung (left) and Kyung-Wha Chung (right). Chung first displayed his musical talent when he began playing the piano at age 4.

The squeaking sounds of instruments being tuned joined with soft laughter and conversation. Soon the auditorium would be filled with music and applause. The Los Angeles Symphony Orchestra[1] was among the best in the nation. Its musicians waited for the conductor[2] who would lead them that night.

The man who walked on stage was not the person everyone expected, however. The orchestra's guest conductor was ill. Almost at the last moment, Myung-Whun Chung (MUNG-HUN CHUNG), a 26-year-old Korean American, was chosen to conduct instead. As he raised his baton[3] to begin the concert, Chung might have wondered himself how this was possible. How could someone so young be conducting this important orchestra? Finding the answer means meeting a remarkable family.

Myung-Whun Chung was born in 1953 in Seoul (SOHL), South Korea, the sixth of seven children. The Korean War, which began in 1950, came to an end the year he was born. Before the war, Chung's father had been a police officer, and his mother, Won-Sook (WAWN-SOOK), had owned the biggest restaurant in Seoul. The family had lived quite comfortably.

When war broke out, however, Communist troops from North Korea poured into South Korea and marched toward Seoul. The Chungs knew that anyone who worked for the South Korean government, as Mr. Chung did, was in great

1. **Symphony Orchestra** (SIHM-fuh-nee OHR-kihs-truh) a large group of musicians who play classical music on string, wind, and percussion instruments

2. **conductor** (kuhn-DUK-tuhr) *n.* the person who leads an orchestra

3. **baton** (buh-TAHN) *n.* a stick used by the conductor to guide an orchestra

danger. Won-Sook helped her husband flee to Japan. She then hastily packed the family's belongings into a truck and, taking the children, drove south to the city of Pusan (POO-sahn). Among the things she took was a large piano. The Chungs loved music, and they weren't about to leave their piano behind–no matter what. (See **Did You Know?** on page 160 for more information on the importance of music to Koreans.)

After the war, when all of the Chungs were able to return to Seoul, they rebuilt their business and resumed a "normal" family life. Normal for the Chungs is exceptional by most standards. Every Chung child started to play music at a very young age. "I just wanted music to be a part of their lives," their mother says. "It was only later that I found out they were talented."

When he was 4 years old, Myung-Whun began to play the piano–and with great skill. By the time he was 7, Myung-Whun had made his concert debut with the Seoul Philharmonic Orchestra. As he approached the piano on the stage, the little boy was greeted in an unusual way. Myung-Whun recalls with a chuckle that "instead of clapping, the audience burst into laughter. They were surprised. *Later* they clapped."

Two of Myung-Whun's older sisters also showed early musical genius. Myung-Wha (MUNG-HAH) began playing the cello[4] with the Seoul Philharmonic at the age of 13. Kyung-Wha (KUNG-HAH) played the violin with the same orchestra when she was only 9 years old. With three children of such rare talent, the Chungs were becoming well-known throughout Korea.

As the children grew older, it became difficult to find musical training for them in Korea. But, in 1961, when Kyung-Wha turned 12, she won a scholarship to study violin at the famous Juilliard School in New York City. Soon after, Myung-Wha joined her sister at Juilliard. By the end of that year, the rest of the family had moved to Seattle, Washington.

---

4. **cello** (CHEHL-oh) *n.* a stringed musical instrument that is larger than a violin and makes a lower sound

Within a few months, the Chungs had opened a Korean restaurant, and Myung-Whun had started high school. Here, he discovered a new world of interests. As a child, he had focused on music. Now, feeling confident about his musical ability, he had the freedom to explore other areas. He went out for sports and played quarterback on his school's football team. All the while, though, he kept up with his music.

After he graduated from high school, Myung-Whun moved to New York City. It was time to give everything to music again. He studied piano and conducting at the Mannes School of Music. The work was very demanding. For the first few years, Chung remembers, "I became depressed[5] because I thought I was behind."

In spite of his doubts, Chung did extremely well. In 1974, when he was 21, he entered the Tchaikovsky (cheye-KAWF-skee) Competition in Moscow. This contest is a kind of Olympics for musicians. Like the Summer and Winter Olympics, this competition is held once every four years, and the most talented young people from around the world compete for prizes. Myung-Whun Chung won second prize in the piano part of the contest. Koreans were proud, but so were Americans. Myung-Whun had become a U.S. citizen in 1973.

Much as he loved playing piano, Chung was becoming interested in the challenges of conducting. A conductor must be able to interpret[6] music so that it sounds fresh and interesting each time it is played. He or she must also know what each of the instruments in the orchestra can do alone and what they can do together.

Even though Chung enjoyed conducting and received training in this field from 1974 to 1978, he was still not sure whether or not he wanted to become a full-time conductor. During these

5. **depressed** (dee-PREHST) *adj.* feeling gloomy or sad

6. **interpret** (ihn-TER-pruht) *v.* to bring out the meaning of; to give one's own idea of

years he maintained a dual[7] career as a conductor and a pianist.

Finally, in 1978, Chung decided to accept the job of Assistant Conductor of the Los Angeles Philharmonic Orchestra. People began to pay close attention to his work as a conductor. As Myung-Whun soon found out, however, the work that the audience sees and appreciates—the leading of the orchestra—is not *all* of the work that a conductor must do. A conductor must manage the business of the orchestra, talk to the press, and also raise money for the orchestra. Chung soon began to tire of these responsibilities. He wanted simply to concentrate on the music.

In 1981, Chung decided to move to Europe. He believed that as a guest conductor in Europe, he could once again focus only on music. He wanted to study the cultures of this continent, where many of the world's great composers have lived and worked. Chung also knew that to gain a worldwide reputation, a musician needed to appear in the great music halls of Europe. By 1984, Chung had worked with most of the major orchestras in Europe.

Chung had also been busy in his private life. He had married, and by 1985, he and his wife Sunyoul (SOON-yohl) had three children—Jin, Sun, and Min. Chung loved being a father and husband. He began to look for opportunities that would allow him to travel less. He thought that finding a permanent position as a conductor might again be a good idea.

In 1989, Chung was named music director of the brand new Bastille (bas-TEEL) Opera in Paris, France. This job was especially challenging because Chung's appointment came just two months before an important date. On July 14, 1989, France would celebrate the 200th anniversary of the French Revolution. The new theater was to be opened for the first time on that day.

Chung threw himself into the preparations. The singers and orchestra needed hours of rehearsal. Yet the building was not quite ready. Musicians sometimes had to dodge bits of falling

---

7. dual (DOO-uhl) *adj.* having two parts

ceiling. The stage machinery did not always work. Nevertheless, a performance was ready for the anniversary celebration. On July 14, great opera singers such as Placido Domingo (PLAH-cee-doh doh-MEEN-goh) performed for the world's leaders. Myung-Whun Chung had made the impossible happen.

Chung has been very successful in leading the young Bastille Opera. Once again, however, he feels burdened by the "business" side of conducting. Myung-Whun looks forward to the day when he can concentrate more on the music itself. Many in the United States hope he will come back home. Wherever he is, however, Chung's universal language—music—will be appreciated. As his sister Myung-Wha says, "It's just music, inborn, ready to speak. It just needs to be brought out."

Did You Know? *Music has always been important to Koreans. The earliest written description of Korean music appears in a Chinese history book from the 3rd century A.D. This book tells of the singing and dancing that took place during certain agricultural festivals, such as those held at the time of the planting and harvesting of crops. It also tells of the use of music to heal the sick and to communicate with the "spirit world." Out of these ancient roots grew Korean folk music, which the government of the Republic of Korea supports by offering courses in schools and granting scholarships to students. Today, Koreans study, play, compose, and enjoy a variety of Western music, including classical, jazz, and rock.*

AFTER YOU READ

EXPLORING YOUR RESPONSES

1. The Chung family took their piano when they fled Seoul. What does this tell you about what the family considered important?

2. In Korean, "Myung" means "bright, shining like a star." Invent a new name for yourself or a friend and explain why you chose it.

3. Music has been a central part of Chung's life. Describe the music you like best and explain why you like it.

4. Myung-Whun Chung has many interests besides music. Do you think it is a good idea to have many interests or to focus on one or two? Explain.

5. Chung was able to accomplish many remarkable things at an early age. What do you think he had to give up in the process?

UNDERSTANDING WORDS IN CONTEXT

Read the following sentences from the biography. Think about what each underlined word means. In your notebook, write what the word means as it is used in the sentence.

1. The [Los Angeles Symphony Orchestra's] musicians waited for the conductor who would lead them that night.

2. As he raised his baton to begin the concert, Chung might have wondered himself how this was possible.

3. The work was very demanding. For the first few years, Chung remembers, "I became depressed because I thought I was behind."

4. A conductor must be able to interpret music so that it sounds fresh and interesting each time it is played.

5. During these years he maintained a <u>dual</u> career as a conductor and a pianist.

RECALLING DETAILS

1. Why did Won-Sook Chung have her children start playing music at a very young age?

2. Describe Myung-Whun's appearance with the Seoul Philharmonic Orchestra when he was 7 years old.

3. What did Myung-Whun Chung do in high school besides practice his music?

4. What parts of conducting does Myung-Whun not like?

5. Describe the challenges Chung faced when he accepted the job with the Bastille Opera.

UNDERSTANDING INFERENCES

In your notebook, write two or three sentences from the biography that support each of the following inferences.

1. The Korean War changed the Chung family's life.

2. The Chung family values music.

3. Learning to be a conductor involves study and hard work.

4. Chung has taken risks in his career.

5. Chung's family is important to him.

INTERPRETING WHAT YOU HAVE READ

1. How might Myung-Whun's upbringing have influenced his attitude toward family life?

2. What would you say Chung looks for most in a job?

3. What do you think Chung hoped to accomplish by going to Europe?

4. "Chung threw himself into his work" when he accepted the job with the Bastille Opera. What does this tell you about Chung's personality?

5. What do you think Myung-Whun Chung would like to do in his career?

ANALYZING QUOTATIONS

Read the following quotation from the biography and answer the questions below.

> As Myung-Whun's sister Myung-Wha says, "It's not a matter of Western or Korean music. It's just music, inborn, ready to speak."

1. What do you think Myung-Wha means when she says music is "inborn, ready to speak"?

2. Do you think Myung-Whun Chung appreciates all kinds of music—rock, rap, folk, and so on? What about his background makes you think so?

3. Make a list of three things that you think people are "born with" and three things that you think people have to learn. Why did you place each of these things in these categories?

THINKING CRITICALLY

1. Why do you think the audience "burst into laughter" when Myung-Whun Chung walked up to the piano for his first public performance?

2. What might Chung have learned from his parents that would make him a good parent?

3. Why do you think Chung wanted to learn to conduct?

4. Why do you think Chung finds the "business" side of conducting so bothersome?

5 Music is often called the universal language. Think of some other "languages" that are universal and that bring people together. What makes these "languages" universal?

CULTURAL CONNECTIONS

Thinking About What People Do

1. All of the performers in this unit had family members who influenced them. Pretend you are a concerned family member of one performer. Write a note to that person telling how you feel about his or her work.

2. With a partner, prepare a radio interview in which one of you acts as the interviewer and the other as one of the performers in this unit. The interview should reveal as much as possible about the performer, including how the person achieved success. Present your radio program to the class.

3. You have been asked to design the cover of the auto-biography for one of the performers in this unit. Think of an appropriate title and design a cover. Present your cover to the class and explain what it reveals about the performer and his or her work.

Thinking About Culture

1. Two of the people in this unit came to the United States because of conflict in their native country. How do you think these conflicts influenced their careers?

2. Compare the ways in which the cultural heritage of two of the performers in this unit affects their work.

3. Some of the performers in this unit felt they did not always "fit in" with others. Discuss the similarities and differences between the barriers two of them experienced.

4. In what ways can a person's cultural heritage be an advantage? Give examples.

Building Research Skills

Work with a partner to complete the following activity.

Choose one of the people discussed in this unit whose work interests you, then imagine that you have decided to do the same kind of work yourself. Make a list of questions about that field. You might begin your list with the following questions:

Hint: The Bibliography at the back of this book lists articles and books to help you begin your research.

☆ What kinds of skills and/or talent do I need for this work?

☆ How would I develop good skills in this field?

☆ How long would it take to develop these skills?

Hint: You might gather more information by interviewing a person from your community who is successful in the field you have researched.

☆ What sacrifices might I have to make to succeed in this field?

☆ What style of living could I expect to have if I pursue work in this field?

Next, use resources in the library to find the answers to your questions. You may wish to develop a chart with the following headings:

Type of career:
Skills:
Type of training required:
Number of years of preparation:

Complete the chart and write several paragraphs about the field of work you have researched.

Create a classroom Career Portfolio that focuses on the careers you and your classmates have selected.

Extending Your Studies

SOCIAL STUDIES **Your task:** *To prepare an oral presentation on communism today.* Communism is a political and an economic system in which all property, goods, and services belong to the government, not to individuals. All people are supposed to share equally whatever is produced in the country. As you read in this unit, many people's lives were affected when the Communists took control of Vietnam and Cambodia.

Until the 1980s, communism had a strong hold in the former Soviet Union, China, and other countries. Work with a small group to choose one country that has been or is still Communist. Go to the library to research the progress of communism in this country. If necessary, ask your social studies teacher or librarian for sources of information. You might begin with the following questions:

☆ What system of government did communism replace?

☆ Why and how did the Communists come to power?

☆ Does communism still exist in this country today?

☆ If it does, do you think a revolution is likely? Explain.

☆ If it does not, how and why did the government change?

Assemble your information and create a group presentation explaining the state of communism in your chosen country.

MUSIC **Your task:** *To make a classical music Top Five.* The type of music that Midori and Myung-Whun Chung perform is called *classical music*. Listen with a partner to a recording of Vivaldi's "Four Seasons," Beethoven's "Ninth Symphony," or Tchaikovsky's "Nutcracker Suite," or ask your librarian to help you make a selection.

Before you listen, make sure you have a pencil and paper and a comfortable place to sit. As you listen, let yourself doodle. Classical music often brings out emotions in people. Do your doodles show how you feel? Do they seem soft and relaxed or are they sharp and pointed? Compare doodles with your partner and discuss how they are similar and different. How did you each respond to the same piece of music?

As a class, discuss your reactions to the pieces of classical music you have chosen. Make a list of Top Five Classics to post for other students in your school.

HEALTH **Your task:** *To assess your heart rate during exercise.* Athletes such as Kristi Yamaguchi have to be in excellent physical condition to meet the demands of their sports. You, too, can work toward a high level of fitness. Begin by figuring out how many minutes you should exercise each week in order to achieve benefits. To do this, choose an aerobic exercise (walking quickly, jogging, or bicycling) and do it for at least 10 minutes. Immediately take your pulse for 10 seconds. (Place your fingers on the side of your neck below your jaw and count the number of pulse beats.) Multiply this number by 6 to figure your exercising pulse rate.

Now determine the percentage of maximum heart rate you are using. Your maximum heart rate is the number of times your heart beats each minute when you are exercising as hard as you can. Your maximum heart rate equals 220 minus your age. (For example, at 13 years old, your maximum heart rate is 207.)

Finally, divide your exercising pulse rate by your maximum heart rate to determine the percentage of your heart rate that you are using. Use the chart below to find out how many minutes of exercise you should do three times a week to improve your level of fitness. Add this exercise time to your weekly schedule.

WRITING WORKSHOP

In Unit 2, you wrote a biographical sketch about a friend. You portrayed that friend through an event you shared. The details you used came from your, or your friend's, memory. For this biography, write a **biographical sketch about someone in your family or community**. To gather information, you will conduct an interview.

PREWRITING

Select a subject: Think about the people in your family—not just those living with you but other relatives as well. Ask your family for ideas that might lead you to an interesting subject. Someone in your community is also a possibility—perhaps someone who has done or achieved something special. In your notebook, jot down three or four names and information about each person. Next, select the person who most interests you, who you think will interest others, and about whom you can gather information.

Gather information: After you choose a subject, jot down questions, ideas, and facts about him or her. In addition to what you know or what you can discover from others, research other sources, such as letters, scrapbooks, and newspaper or magazine articles. Record your findings in your notebook.

Arrange an interview: Arrange to interview your subject or someone who knows the subject well.

Organize your questions: Read through all the information you have recorded about your subject, then write down questions you will ask him or her. Focus on an important event in that person's life and what he or she learned from it. Here are a few ideas for questions:

☆ What is one important, or even the most important, event in your life?

☆ Where did the event take place?

☆ What happened?

☆ What did you say and do?

☆ Who else was there?

☆ What did he or she do or say?

☆ How did you feel?

☆ What did you learn?

☆ Why was this event important to you?

☆ Would you want to go through this event again? Why or why not?

Conduct your interview: Ask the questions you have prepared, avoiding questions that can be answered with "yes" or "no." Be alert to your subject's answers so that if he or she mentions an interesting fact, ask for more information. You do not have to ask only the questions you prepared. Take notes or record the interview, then thank your subject and offer to show him or her the sketch when you finish.

Organizing: Sort through your notes, then decide on a main idea—the most important thing you learned from your subject. Underline details you will use. Then, in your notebook, write your subject's name, the event, and what he or she learned. For example:

Subject: Great Aunt Jessie
Event: When she got her college diploma at age 60
What I learned: It's never too late to achieve a goal.

DRAFTING

Once you have organized your notes and decided on a main idea, begin drafting your sketch.

The Opening: The opening should introduce the person and event and hold the reader's interest. For example:

> *My Great Aunt Jessie had invited friends, relatives, and even the mail carrier to what she says is, "The biggest event in my life—so far."*

The Body: Here you will bring your subject to life through your description of the event. Remember that by showing what your subject says and does and by describing how he or she looks, thinks, and feels, you let the reader "meet" your subject.

The Closing: By the end of your biographical sketch, the reader should be able to "see" your subject and understand what he or she learned from the event. In our example the writer learned that it is never too late to achieve a goal.

> *At the graduation party, Ernie, the mail carrier, said to Aunt Jessie, "Well, I guess you can take it easy now. No more studying."*
>
> *Aunt Jessie laughed. "Getting this degree was great. Now I feel like I can get another one. Next fall I'm starting on my master's degree!"*

REVISING

Put your biographical sketch aside for a day or two. Then, with the help of another student who will act as your editor, evaluate and revise your work. See the directions for writers and student editors below.

Directions to Writers: Before you give your sketch to a student editor, ask yourself the following questions:

☆ Does the opening hold the reader's interest?

☆ Do I give enough details to describe the event?

☆ Am I *showing*, not *telling*, the reader what happened?

☆ Does the dialogue sound natural?

☆ Does the ending sum up what my subject learned and leave the reader with a lasting impression?

Make notes for your next draft or revise your work before you give it to your student editor. Then ask your student editor to read your work. Listen carefully to his or her suggestions. If they seem helpful, use them to improve your writing when you revise your work.

Directions for Student Editors: Read the work carefully and respectfully, remembering that your purpose is to help the writer do his or her best work. Keep in mind that an editor should always make positive, helpful comments that point to specific parts of the essay. After you read the work, use the following questions to help direct your comments:

☆ What do I like most about the biographical sketch?

☆ Can I see the person or event in my mind?

☆ Has the writer made the subject come alive?

☆ What would I like to know more about?

PROOFREADING

When you are satisfied that your work says what you want it to say, check it carefully for errors in spelling, punctuation, grammar, and capitalization. Then make a neat, final copy of your work.

PUBLISHING

After you revise your sketch, you are ready to publish it. Illustrate your finished copy with drawings, a collage, or photos. Make your biographical sketch available for other students to read in a library of Very Important People.

ASIAN AMERICANS IN THE SCIENCES AND PUBLIC SERVICE

This unit will introduce you to six Asian Americans who work to improve human health and understanding in government, medicine, computer technology, and even the study of the stars. As you read, think about the qualities necessary to succeed in these fields. Think, too, about how their cultural heritage has affected their life and work.

Chinese American inventor **An Wang** designed his machines only after watching people work and learning how they could work more easily and more happily. "People don't want technology; they want solutions to problems," Wang observed.

Through a career in law and government, Japanese American **Patsy Takemoto Mink** has worked hard to protect people's rights. "Possibly the highest achievement is to find a place in life that permits one to be of service to [others]," she says.

Subrahmanyan Chandrasekhar (soo-BRAH-muhn-yahn chuhn-druh-SHAY-kuhr), born in India, has spent his life studying the stars. He says, "If I cannot pursue a subject in earnest, I would rather not make the effort at all."

Chinese American medical researcher **Constance Tom Noguchi** (nuh-GOOT-chee) says, "It's always fun when [experiments] work out the way you expect. It's even more fun when you get unexpected results."

Cancer researcher **Susumu Tone-gawa** (soo-SOO-moo tahn-uh-GAH-wuh), who is Japanese American, won the Nobel Prize for Medicine in 1987. Co-worker Nancy Hopkins has said, "Susumu is really a spectacular scientist."

Filipino American surgeon **Juan Montero** (HWAHN mohn-TER-oh) marvels, "It never ceases to amaze me what [a] thin line separates life from death—often so thin as the mark of a knife blade."

As you read, consider how the person's work has helped to solve problems in the world. Take note of how each person feels about what he or she does. Also look for information that will give you a picture of the subject as a person.

AN WANG

An Wang, Chinese American inventor, delivers a speech. Throughout his career, Wang followed the ancient Chinese philosphy of Confucianism, which stresses human kindness and respect.

No more procrastinating.[1] It is time to work on that story. As the reporter types, her thoughts appear neatly on the screen of the word processor. Did she misspell a word or leave something out? She just presses a few keys and fixes her errors or adds a new thought. The computer makes it easy for her to change her mind as often as she likes. When she is done, she presses a few more keys and her story is neatly printed out.

The life of a writer has certainly changed. In millions of offices, schools, and homes around the world, computers now let people work with an ease and speed that was unimaginable just 50 years ago. An Wang, a Chinese American inventor and businessman, helped lead this "computer revolution."

An Wang was born in Shanghai (SHANG-HEYE), China, in 1920. His name means "peaceful king." But there was little peace in China then—and there was no king. Instead, rival leaders fought for power, and Japan prepared to invade China.

Trying to avoid the fighting, An's family moved to a city called Kun San (KUN SAHN) when he was six years old. There, he went to a grammar school where his father taught English. But because the school had no earlier grades, An was enrolled as a third grader, and he often had difficulty keeping up with the older students. He says that it felt "like being thrown in the water when you don't know how to swim. You either learn how to swim—and fast—or you sink!"

An's favorite subjects were always math and science. But there was more to his education. Wang's grandmother told him about Confucius (kuhn-FYOO-shuhs), an ancient Chinese thinker. Confucius taught loyalty to one's family and community. He also

---

1. **procrastinating** (proh-KRAS-tuh-nayt-ihng) *v.* putting off doing something

stressed the importance of treating people fairly and living peacefully. (See **Did You Know?** on page 179 for more information on Confucius.) Years later, when Wang ran a large company, he would apply[2] the lessons of Confucius.

At 16, he began college, where he studied electrical engineering and communications. Life was not all books, though. Wang enjoyed politics, and served as class president for four years. He also enjoyed sports. But, being younger and smaller than most of his classmates, he was not very successful in team sports. Wang recalls that in soccer, he was more "target" than "goalie." But he excelled at table tennis, in which skill is more important than size.

Meanwhile, the Japanese invaded Shanghai in 1937, and by 1939, World War II had erupted.[3] After graduating, Wang volunteered to build radios for the Chinese army. However, it was hard to get radio parts. So, Wang learned how to make do with what he had. Already, he was becoming an innovator.[4]

After the war, Wang decided that he could learn more about new technologies in the United States. He was accepted at Harvard University, where he soon got his Master of Science degree. In 1948, he earned a Ph.D. in physics,[5] also from Harvard.

One of the most important inventions of the war years was the computer. Wang was fascinated by its power and started working at the Harvard Computation Laboratory. He assisted Dr. Howard Aiken (AY-kuhn), who had built one of the first true computers in the United States, the Mark I.

The Mark I was huge. It filled an entire room, but for all its size, it was very slow. It used electric switches to store numbers. When the computer flipped a switch one way, it stood for the digit 1. Flipped the other way, it stood for 0. If you put enough

---

2. **apply** (uh-PLEYE) *v.* to put to some practical use

3. **erupted** (ee-RUHPT-ihd) *v.* broke out or burst forth

4. **innovator** (IHN-uh-vayt-uhr) *n.* a person who creates new products or ideas

5. **physics** (FIHZ-ihks) *n.* the branch of science that deals with basic properties of matter and energy

1's and 0's together, you could store any number. The problem was that the switches took too long to flip back and forth.

Wang soon realized that computers would be much faster if there were no moving parts. Instead, he figured, the electrical signals themselves could stand for numbers. Unlike the slow switches, electricity could move at the speed of light. But coming up with a good idea and actually making something happen are two different things.

Wang found that by passing electricity through a wire, a tiny doughnut-shaped magnet, called the core, could be magnetized[6] in one of two ways. One way could stand for 1, and the other for 0. Wang soon presented the world with a machine that could solve complicated mathematical problems in a few minutes.

Wang's magnetic cores became the most important method of computer memory from about 1950, when he was barely 30 years old, to 1970. Eventually, core memories were replaced by the much faster memory "chips" in use today.

By 1951, Harvard had stopped doing basic computer research. Wang saw this as an opportunity to start his own computer business. With $600, he started Wang Laboratories. He was taking a big risk, though—not only because many businesses fail but also because he had new personal responsibilities.

In 1949, Wang married Lorraine Chu (CHOO), who was also from Shanghai. By the time An decided to leave Harvard—and a regular salary—he and Lorraine had a son, Frederick. Could Wang's new business make enough money to support the family? Would he face discrimination, as his Chinese friends feared?

But An Wang had a special confidence. "I have always felt intense pride in the historical depth of Chinese culture. A Chinese [person] can never outgrow his roots. Ancient ideas such as Confucianism are as [important] today as they were [2500] years ago. . . . I had also mastered [the sciences] that have been the special strength of Western societies. In other words, I felt I had succeeded in the West's own terms."

---

6. **magnetized** (MAG-nuh-teyezd) *v.* made into a magnet

Wang's company made and sold memory cores. It also produced new kinds of calculating machines for scientists and engineers. The man who had once built radios out of scrap material was now designing and building high quality machines at a low price. After only six months, Wang was making more money on his own than he had made at Harvard.

Wang–the entrepreneur,[7] the business "whiz"–never stopped inventing. He designed an electronic scoreboard for New York's Shea Stadium. He also designed a special typewriter that automatically sets newspaper type in columns. Wang was always looking for ways to make life easier and work fun.

In the 1960s, Wang turned to making powerful compact calculators. One reason Wang's products sold so well is that he understood people's needs. Wang asked questions, and he observed people at work. He discovered that "people don't want technology, they want solutions to problems."

Always ready for a challenge, Wang began making machines that would do for words what his calculators had done for numbers. Wang's first word processors, which came out in the early 1970s, were little more than fancy electric typewriters. But Wang knew he could design something far better.

Wang again looked at the way people *did* office work. How could boring tasks be made easy and fun? "I felt secretarial work was real drudgery.[8] If you made typing mistakes, you would have to retype the entire document. So why not put the information on a screen where it could be easily erased and edited?" Wang made it sound so simple. Offices around the world were forever changed by the Wang word processor.

Through the 1970s and early 1980s, Wang Labs made tremendous profits. But then, smaller, cheaper personal computers, made by companies such as IBM and Apple, came on the market. These computers were useful as word processors, but

7. **entrepreneur** (ahn-truh-pruh-NER) *n.* a person who takes risks in starting a new business

8. **drudgery** (DRUJ-uhr-ee) *n.* work that is hard and boring

they could also be used for a number of other jobs. To make matters worse, the economy took a downward turn. Wang Labs began to lose money.

In characteristic style, Wang went directly to his customers and talked to them about their needs. He then reorganized Wang Labs and put it back on the road to success. In 1986, it won a U.S. Air Force contract worth almost half a billion dollars.

Meanwhile, Wang continued to follow the teachings of Confucius. He donated computers to help run shelters for homeless people, and he built a factory to provide jobs for the poor in Boston's Chinatown. Wang also helped fund a student exchange program between the United States and China. For his many efforts, Wang was awarded the Medal of Liberty at the relighting of the Statue of Liberty in 1986.

When An Wang died of cancer in 1990, he was one of the wealthiest people in the United States. But it was never obvious. Rather, he was known for his "astounding" intelligence, his openness, and his simplicity.

Did You Know? *An Wang's approach to life was influenced by the ancient Chinese thinker Confucius, who lived from about 551 to 479 B.C. Confucius believed that all people had within them the desire and ability to be good and to live an honorable life. But goodness in itself meant little to Confucius. To him, the important thing was to be kind to others. He called the perfect relationship between people jen, a relationship based on equality, friendliness, and generosity. Confucius taught that if every relationship—between parent and child, wife and husband, teacher and student, and leader and subject, as well as between friends—had these qualities, the society as a whole would be just and peaceful. In other words, a society reflects the way individuals treat one another. If people treat one another with kindness and respect, the world is at peace.*

AFTER YOU READ

EXPLORING YOUR RESPONSES

1. An Wang said his first year of school felt like "being thrown in the water when you don't know how to swim." Do you like to learn in a "sink or swim" situation, or do you prefer to learn gradually?

2. Many centuries ago, Confucius taught the importance of treating people fairly. Describe three ways in which you think people can treat one another fairly.

3. Wang helped further the cause of peace and justice in many ways, including donating computers to homeless shelters. How might you further this cause?

4. An Wang was successful because he understood how people worked. Think of a job in your home, classroom, or community. What might help people do this task more easily?

5. Imagine you could start a business of your own. What would that business be? Why did you choose it?

UNDERSTANDING WORDS IN CONTEXT

Read the following sentences from the biography. Think about what each underlined word means. In your notebook, write what the word means as it is used in the sentence.

1. No more procrastinating. It is time to work on that story.

2. So, Wang learned to make do with what he had. Already, he was becoming an innovator.

3. [Confucius] also stressed the importance of treating people fairly and living peacefully. Years later, when Wang ran a large company, he would apply the lessons of Confucius.

4. Wang found that by passing electricity through a wire, a tiny doughnut-shaped magnet, called the core, could be magnetized in one of two ways.

5. Wang–the <u>entrepreneur</u>, the business "whiz"–never stopped inventing.

RECALLING DETAILS

1. What were Wang's favorite subjects in school?

2. What did Wang learn from his grandmother?

3. How did Wang feel about starting his own business?

4. What made the Mark I computer so slow?

5. In what ways did Wang contribute to society?

UNDERSTANDING INFERENCES

In your notebook, write two or three sentences from the biography that support each of the following inferences.

1. An Wang's Chinese background affected his life and career.

2. Wang was willing to take risks.

3. Education contributed to Wang's success.

4. Wang was always thinking of new and better ways of doing things.

5. Helping people was important to Wang.

INTERPRETING WHAT YOU HAVE READ

1. How did the teachings of Confucius influence Wang?

2. How do you think building radios during World War II affected Wang's later career?

3. Why do you think Wang left Harvard to start his own computer business?

4. What skills and personal characteristics helped An Wang become a success?

5. Why did Wang Laboratories begin losing money in the 1980s?

ANALYZING QUOTATIONS

Read the following quotation from the biography and answer the questions below.

> *"I have always felt an intense pride in the historical depth of Chinese culture. A Chinese [person] can never outgrow his roots. Ancient ideas such as Confucianism are as [important] today as they were [2500] years ago."*

1. What do you think Wang meant when he said a person can "never outgrow his roots"?
2. In what ways did An Wang practice Confucianism?
3. Name something from your own cultural background of which you are proud—an idea, a value, a saying, a custom, or a tradition. Explain why it is important to you.

THINKING CRITICALLY

1. Why do you think Wang's grandmother told him about the teachings of Confucius?
2. Wang wanted to sell a large number of machines at a low price. Some other companies wanted to sell fewer machines at a higher price. What do you think are the good and bad points of each kind of business?
3. Wang said, "People don't want technology, they want solutions to problems." Name a problem that you or someone you know faces and suggest how technology might solve it.
4. An Wang's name means "peaceful king." In what ways do you think Wang lived up to his name?
5. Wang's grandmother taught him to be loyal to one's family and community and to treat people fairly. If you could teach a child only two things, what would you teach and why?

PATSY TAKEMOTO MINK

Patsy Takemoto Mink, a U.S representative from Hawaii, and former Congresswoman Bella Abzug (left) enjoy the activity at the 1980 Democratic Convention. As a Japanese American, Mink believes that people should be treated equally regardless of their cultural backgrounds.

When Patsy Takemoto (TAH-kay-moh-toh) Mink ran for election to the U.S. House of Representatives in 1964, she followed an old Japanese custom to bring good luck. She bought a *daruma* (dah-RU-mah) doll, which has no eyes. After Mink won the Democratic primary election[1] in her home state of Hawaii, she painted in one eye. Only after she won the general election did she paint in the other one. (See **Did You Know?** on page 188 for more information about daruma dolls.)

Though Patsy Mink is proud of and knowledgeable about her Japanese heritage, she is uneasy about being labeled "Japanese American." Mink believes that people's similarities should be emphasized and that people should be treated equally. "I just live for the day when people will look at me and simply call me an American. . . . I feel, act, and live like any other American the country over." Mink would fight throughout her political career for just such equality.

Mink agrees, though, that her perspective[2] on issues is special. She says, "I bring to Congress . . . a Hawaiian background of tolerance[3] and equality that can contribute a great deal to better understanding between races."

People of different cultures have lived together in Hawaii for many years. When Mink was first elected, there were as many Japanese Americans as white Americans in Hawaii. Together, they made up 64 percent of the state's population. The remaining

1. **primary election** (PREYE-mehr-ee ee-LEHK-shuhn) an election to choose the candidate who will represent a particular political party in a later election
2. **perspective** (puhr-SPEHK-tihv) *n.* a person's point of view or understanding
3. **tolerance** (TAHL-uhr-uhns) *n.* willingness to respect other people's beliefs and practices

36 percent included people of Filipino, native Hawaiian, Chinese, and African descent. Patsy's family, the Takemotos, for example, have lived in Hawaii since the 1880s.

When Patsy Takemoto was born on the island of Maui (MOW-ee), in 1927, Hawaii was a territory[4] of the United States. It did not become a state until 1959. But the people of Hawaii did have a non-voting delegate in Washington, D.C. They also had many cultural and economic ties with the U.S. mainland before statehood.

When she was young, Patsy wanted to be a doctor. "Our family physician had been one of my heroes," she recalls. When she went to the University of Hawaii in Honolulu in 1944, she took pre-medical courses.

Once in college, however, Patsy found another hero, Franklin D. Roosevelt, who was the U.S. President from 1933 to 1945. To her, Roosevelt stood for the tolerance she had learned to value as a child. "It seemed to me that possibly the highest achievement is to find a place in life that permits one to be of service to his fellow men."

Patsy Takemoto became interested in politics in high school, where she was student body president. Her interest in politics and a related field, law, reappeared in college. In 1948, Patsy entered the University of Chicago School of Law because of what she calls a "lucky accident." Each year the school admitted a certain number of students from foreign countries. "Some idiot there thought Hawaii was a foreign country, so I was accepted," Mink explains with a smile.

While at Chicago, Patsy Takemoto met John Mink, a geologist.[5] They were married in 1951. Later, they had a daughter, Gwendolyn. A lawyer, a wife, and a mother, Patsy Mink and her family moved back to Hawaii in 1952.

---

4. **territory** (TEHR-uh-tawr-ee) *n.* a part of a country that has some rights, but not as many as a fully recognized part, such as a state

5. **geologist** (jee-AHL-uh-jihst) *n.* a scientist who studies rocks and minerals to learn about the earth

Mink was only the second Asian American woman to practice law in Hawaii. At first she tried to join one of the large law firms in Honolulu, on the island of Oahu (oh–AH–hoo). None of them would hire her, however, because she was a woman. "Stay home and take care of your child," they told her. Far from taking their advice, Mink set up her own law practice.

Mink also became active in politics, starting a branch of the Young Democrats in 1954. Then, in 1956, she was elected to the Hawaii House of Representatives, and, in 1958, to the Hawaii Senate.

In 1959, when Hawaii became a state, Patsy Mink ran for a seat in the U.S. House of Representatives, but she did not win the Democratic primary. Undaunted,[6] she tried again in 1964, and this time she won. At 36, Mink became the first woman from Hawaii to serve in the U.S. Congress.

Political campaigns cost a great deal of money. Many candidates either are wealthy or have wealthy supporters. Patsy Mink's campaign was paid for entirely by small amounts of money from the many people who wanted her to win. All her campaign workers were volunteers. Her husband was her campaign manager. It was, some might say, a "small–time operation"—but it worked.

Once Mink got to Congress, she was elected again and again. In 1966, she won by the highest percentage of votes in the state's history. By 1968, Mink was among the top ten vote-getters in the U.S. House of Representatives.

Deeply committed to educational equality, Mink was appointed to the important House Education and Labor Committee in the early 1970s—in her words "only after the hardest and most intense campaign of my life." Some members of the committee disagreed with her views on education. What Patsy Mink wanted was an educational system that treated girls and boys equally, that didn't teach "girls do this best, and boys do that best."

---

6. **undaunted** (uhn-DAWNT-ihd) *adj.* not afraid or discouraged

Some of Mink's other ideas were also unpopular in Congress. She was strongly against the Vietnam War, in which the United States was involved from 1964 to 1975. Many people agreed with her and protested against the war. Some members of Congress wanted these protesters punished severely. Mink defended their rights: "America is not a country which needs to punish its dissenters[7] to preserve its honor," she said. "Its strength lies in . . . one common belief, that of the importance of freedom as the essence[8] of our country."

Mink's political career took a slight detour in 1971. A number of supporters asked her to enter the 1972 Oregon Presidential primary. She knew she would not get the nomination, but she had a message to get out—women are in politics for keeps. Mink got only 2 percent of the vote, but she was convinced that "there'll be a woman Vice President sooner than might otherwise have been the case."

In 1976, Patsy Mink decided that she would not run for Congress again. Instead, she took another important government position as Assistant Secretary for Oceans and International Environmental and Scientific Affairs (OES). Mink's job was to make treaties with other nations concerning the world's environmental problems.

While at OES, Patsy Mink worked on a number of serious issues, including acid rain. She was involved in trying to prevent acid rain and to correct its effects. Mink also worked on treaties to protect Antarctica and the sea surrounding it. Under her leadership the world's major nations agreed that all countries could send scientists there, but none could claim land or strip Antarctica of its natural resources.

Patsy Mink was with the OES for about a year and a half. She quit in May 1978 because she felt that the government was not letting her do her job, that it lacked commitment to the

7. **dissenters** (dih–SEHNT-uhrz) *n. pl.* people who disagree with a belief, idea, or policy; protesters
8. **essence** (EHS-uhns) *n.* the most important or basic quality of something

environment. Her chances to take part in important policy decisions, she said, "were far more limited than I had expected."

Mink then returned to Hawaii, where she served on the Honolulu City Council from 1983 to 1988. But she again felt the urge to fight for what she thinks is right on the national level. In 1990, she ran for the U.S. House of Representatives and was reelected. After more than 35 years of valuable public service, Patsy Mink does not have to rely on luck anymore for victory. She can rely on her record.

Did You Know? *People in Japan often buy a daruma doll when they start a new project. The doll has no eyes, but its owner paints in one eye at the beginning of the project and makes a wish. When the project succeeds or the wish comes true, he or she then paints in the second eye. Patsy Mink did not tell anyone about her wish. "It's really a very private thing," she said later. "Like when you see a falling star, you don't tell everyone what you're wishing." But it is probably safe to say that Mink wished for the opportunity to serve her state and country.*

EXPLORING YOUR RESPONSES

1. Patsy Takemoto Mink's heroes helped her decide on a career. What effect has a hero had on your life or on the life of a friend?

2. Mink's wish to win the 1964 election to the U.S. House of Representatives came true. What do you think people need to do to "make wishes come true"?

3. Mink comes from a state where many different cultures live together peacefully. Suggest some ways in which groups of people can live together peacefully.

4. Patsy Mink kept fighting to achieve her goals, even when that angered some people. Why do you think achieving a goal sometimes means angering others?

5. Mink believes in the importance of freedom and fairness. In what ways might being fair to people increase the amount of freedom everyone has? Explain.

UNDERSTANDING WORDS IN CONTEXT

Read the following sentences from the biography. Think about what each underlined word means. In your notebook, write what the word means as it is used in the sentence.

1. "I bring to Congress . . . a Hawaiian background of tolerance and equality that can contribute a great deal to better understanding between races."

2. Mink agrees, though, that her perspective on issues is special [because] . . . people of many cultures have lived together peacefully in Hawaii for many centuries.

3. In 1959, Patsy Mink ran for a seat in the U.S. House of Representatives, but she did not win. . . . Undaunted, she tried again in 1964, and this time she won.

4. Some members of Congress wanted [the Vietnam War] protesters punished severely. Mink defended their rights: "America is not a country which needs to punish its dissenters," she said.

5. "[The United States'] strength lies in . . . one common belief, that of the importance of freedom as the essence of our country."

RECALLING DETAILS

1. What is Patsy Mink's attitude toward her Japanese heritage?

2. Why did a Honolulu law firm refuse to hire Mink?

3. Who were Patsy Mink's heroes?

4. What was Mink's position on the Vietnam War?

5. What did Mink do to protect the environment when she worked at OES?

UNDERSTANDING INFERENCES

In your notebook, write two or three sentences from the biography that support each of the following inferences.

1. Patsy Takemoto Mink was popular with voters.

2. Mink values education for herself and others.

3. Mink is concerned about the environment.

4. Mink believes people should be treated fairly.

5. Once elected, politicians still have to fight for what they believe.

INTERPRETING WHAT YOU HAVE READ

1. Why might Mink have worked to change the ways boys and girls were taught in school during the 1960s?

2. Mink was elected many times to Congress. What does this tell you about her effectiveness?

3. How might being a woman have shaped Mink's perspective on issues?

4. Why might Mink want to take many small campaign contributions rather than rely on a few big contributions?

5. How might Mink's unsuccessful run in the 1972 Democratic Presidential Primary help other women run for the Presidency or Vice-Presidency?

ANALYZING QUOTATIONS

Read the following quotation from the biography and answer the questions below.

> *"It seemed to me that possibly the highest achievement is to find a place in life that permits one to be of service to his fellow men."*

1. What do you think Mink means by being "of service" to others?

2. How does Patsy Mink's life show a dedication to service?

3. What do you think is the "highest achievement"? Explain.

THINKING CRITICALLY

1. How do you think Mink's rejection by the large law firms in Hawaii affected her career?

2. How do you think Patsy Mink feels about women in politics and why?

3. Why might Mink have chosen to defend those who could not speak for themselves?

4. Not all of Mink's ideas were popular. Do you think it is possible for a leader to get everyone to agree with his or her ideas? Explain.

5. Throughout her career, Mink has worked for social and political equality and for a better environment. Name two ways individuals can help achieve these goals.

SUBRAHMANYAN CHANDRASEKHAR

Subrahmanyan Chandrasekhar, Indian American physicist, sits at
the base of the Henry Moore sculpture *Nuclear Energy* in Chicago. In
1983, Chandrasekhar won the Nobel Prize in physics for his research
on black holes.

The ship sailed on peacefully as evening came. Overhead was a "sea" that was even deeper than the one on which the ship was sailing. It was a sea of stars.

One of the ship's passengers was Subrahmanyan Chandrasekhar (soo–BRAH–muhn–yahn chuhn–druh–SHAY–kuhr). At 19, he was traveling from his home in India to England, where he would study astronomy[1] at Cambridge University.

"Chandra," as his friends call him, was not just a romantic[2] star-gazer, dreamily making wishes. He was thinking about the stars. What is a star made of? How does it come into being? What happens to a star when it gets old? Does it explode?

Chandra would ask and answer questions like these for many years. More than 50 years later, Chandra's work would win him the Nobel Prize in physics, the highest honor in science.

Chandra was born in Lahore (lah–HOHR), India, in 1910. When he was five years old, his relatives gathered together to celebrate a holiday called Vijayadasami (vee–jah–YAH–dah–sah–mee), which marks the beginning of a child's formal education. Chandra's family made offerings to the god and goddess of learning. After a dinner of celebration, Chandra and his father sat side by side, and sand was spread out in front of them. Each guest wrote a message in the sand, wishing Chandra future success. To end the ceremony, Chandra wrote the first few letters of the Tamil[3] alphabet in the sand.

Described as "unbearably mischievous[4] as a toddler, Chandra was now ready to learn. But Chandra and his brothers and sisters

1. **astronomy** (uh–STRAHN–uh–mee) *n.* the study of stars and planets
2. **romantic** (roh–MAN–tihk) *adj.* idealistic; valuing the emotions over reason
3. **Tamil** (TAM–uhl) *n.* a language spoken by many people in South India and Sri Lanka, an island near India
4. **mischievous** (MIHS–chuh–vuhs) *adj.* teasing; full of tricks and pranks

did not go to school at first. Instead, their parents taught them at home. Most of the schools for Indian children did not teach English, and people who wanted good jobs with the government had to speak and write English well. (See **Did You Know?** on page 196 for more information on the British influence on Indian education.)

When Chandra was ready for college, he and his father disagreed about what Chandra should study. Chandra wanted to study mathematics. One of his boyhood heroes was Srinivasa Ramanujan (SRIHN-ih-vah-sah rah-MAH-nuh-juhn), a brilliant Indian mathematician. Chandra's father, however, wanted the young man to study physics.

Chandra had nothing against physics. Indeed, Chandra's other scientific hero was his uncle Chandrasekhara Raman (RAH-muhn), a famous physicist.[5] But Chandra knew that his father's motive[6] was job security for his son. He wanted Chandra to get a high position in the British-run Indian Civil Service. Chandra, however, did not want to work for the government. His mother took his side. "You should do what you like. Don't listen to him [your father]," she said.

In a sense, Chandra compromised.[7] He went to Madras University and studied physics, as his father wanted. But Chandra planned to be a scientist, not a government worker.

At the university, Chandra read about the exciting work of two British astronomers, Arthur Eddington and Ralph Fowler. After years of research, these two had concluded that all stars sooner or later become "white dwarfs" or very old stars that no longer make much light because they have run out of hydrogen gas. Eventually, they concluded, gravity causes the star to reduce in size and brightness.

Chandra decided to study astronomy as well as physics so he could learn more about these ideas. He also decided to go to

5. **physicist** (FIHZ-ih-sihst) *n.* a scientist who studies matter and energy

6. **motive** (MOHT-ihv) *n.* intention; the reason for doing something

7. **compromised** (KAHM-pruh-meyezd) *v.* reached a solution that considers both sides of an issue

England. During the long ocean voyage in 1930, Chandra studied Eddington's ideas and concluded that Eddington was right about small stars, those about the size of our sun.

But what about bigger stars? The stronger gravity of a big star would pull harder on the star's gas, he thought. When the gas reached the center of the star, parts of it would be moving almost as fast as light. The great scientist Albert Einstein (EYEN-steyen) had worked out mathematical equations[8] to describe what happens when things move that fast. When Chandra used Einstein's equations, he found that big stars could not turn into white dwarfs. It seemed that gravity would make them shrink until they were much smaller than white dwarfs, until they turned into what would later be named "black holes."

While at Cambridge University, Chandra studied with both Eddington and Fowler. Eddington could not believe that some stars might keep shrinking forever. "There ought to be a law of nature to prevent a star from behaving in this absurd[9] way," the older scientist insisted. Nevertheless, Chandra excelled as a student and received his Ph.D. in 1933.

When Eddington, one of the world's leading astronomers, spoke, people listened. It took years before other astronomers would accept Chandra's ideas about black holes, mostly because Eddington had disagreed with them. Chandra has mixed feelings about his problems with Eddington. If Eddington had agreed with Chandra, astronomers might have learned much earlier about black holes. As it turned out, it was not until the 1960s that scientists began to investigate black holes: these are stars that gravity has packed so tightly that even their light cannot escape.

On the other hand, Chandra wonders, "Eddington's praise could make one very famous in astronomy. But I really do not know how I would have reacted to the temptation, to the glamour." Something to fight against, Chandra seems to say, can help rather than hurt.

---

8. **equations** (ee-KWAY-zhuhnz) *n. pl.* mathematical statements that describe an event or thing with numbers

9. **absurd** (ab-SERD) *adj.* clearly wrong or unreasonable; very silly

In 1937, Chandra and Lalitha moved to the United States, where he joined the Department of Astronomy at the University of Chicago. His fellow astronomers were amazed by Chandra's work habits. Once Chandra chose a problem, he would work on it every day until he had an answer—even if it took years. Only when he thought he understood everything about the problem would he write a paper, in which he would lay out his ideas step by step.

During the 1940s and 1950s, Chandra studied how energy moves inside the heart of a star and how galaxies, or large systems of stars, "behave." He discovered that galaxies like our own Milky Way act like huge magnets. He showed that their pull can be strong enough to bend stars out of shape.

Chandra did much of his work on black holes from about 1974 to 1983, the year he won the Nobel Prize. He was 73 years old at the time. Now in his 80s, Chandra continues his work at the University of Chicago. He also continues to gaze at, and ask questions about, the stars.

> **Did You Know?** *The period when the British ruled India, from 1757 to 1947, is called the Raj (RAHJ). The Hindi word* raj *means "rule" or "regime" in English. During this period, and even after, British influence on India was tremendous. Every aspect of Indian life was affected—from what people wore to what they learned. Powerful and wealthy Indians spoke English, and many were educated in England. Chandra's parents were not wealthy, but they could afford to give their children what educated Indians of the time considered the best start in life—an English education.*

AFTER YOU READ

EXPLORING YOUR RESPONSES

1. Before Chandra went to the Hindu High School, he was taught at home. What do you think are the pros and cons of learning at home?

2. Chandra disagreed with his father on what he should study in college. Why do parents and children sometimes disagree on what to study and what career to choose?

3. At Madras University, Chandra read about discoveries in astronomy. What kind of discoveries would you be most interested in reading about and why?

4. Arthur Eddington disagreed strongly with Chandra's ideas about stars. How might you have responded to this disagreement if you were in Chandra's place?

5. Chandra had the ability to concentrate completely on a problem. What do you think he gained and lost by this ability?

UNDERSTANDING WORDS IN CONTEXT

Read the following sentences from the biography. Think about what each underlined word means. In your notebook, write what the word means as it is used in the sentence.

1. "Chandra" . . . was not just a romantic star-gazer, dreamily making wishes. He was asking himself many hard questions about the stars and space.

2. To keep Chandra's inquisitive mind occupied, his father also hired private teachers.

3. In a sense, Chandra compromised. He went to Madras University and studied physics, as his father wanted. But Chandra planned to be a scientist, not a government worker.

4. But Chandra knew that his father's <u>motive</u> was job security for his son. He wanted Chandra to get a high position in the British-run Indian Civil Service.

5. [Eddington] could not believe that some stars might keep shrinking forever. "There ought to be a law of nature to prevent a star from behaving in this <u>absurd</u> way."

RECALLING DETAILS

1. Why did Chandra's parents begin their children's education at home?

2. What was Chandra's favorite school subject?

3. What did Chandra and his father disagree about?

4. What was Eddington's reaction to Chandra's ideas about black holes?

5. Describe the work that earned Chandra the Nobel Prize for physics.

UNDERSTANDING INFERENCES

In your notebook, write two or three sentences from the biography that support each of the following inferences.

1. Chandra was curious about the universe.

2. Education was very important to Chandra's family.

3. Chandra tried to please his father as well as himself.

4. Chandra was a hard worker.

5. People are not always ready to accept the truth or ideas that are different from their own.

INTERPRETING WHAT YOU HAVE READ

1. Why do you think it was so important to Chandra's family that he learn English?

2. Chandra's mother told him, "You should do what you like." Did Chandra take her advice? Explain.

3. How did Chandra's and Eddington's views about stars differ?

4. What does the Vijayadasami celebration tell you about Indian values?

5. Why do you think it sometimes takes so long to make a scientific "discovery"?

ANALYZING QUOTATIONS

Read the following quotation from the biography and answer the questions below.

> "Eddington's praise could make one very famous in astronomy. But I really do not know how I would have reacted to the temptation, to the glamour."

1. The second sentence of this quote suggests a fear or concern. What do you think that fear might be?

2. If Eddington's praise could make a person famous, what could his rejection do?

3. Surprisingly, praise can sometimes get in the way of a person's achieving all he or she can. Why do you think this might be?

THINKING CRITICALLY

1. Why do you think Chandra chose not to pursue a career in the Indian Civil Service as his father wished?

2. Why do you think people were more willing to accept Eddington's idea about stars than Chandra's ideas?

3. What do you think might have happened to Chandra's career if Eddington had immediately accepted Chandra's ideas about what happens when big stars shrink?

4. What qualities do you think are important for a scientist to have? Why?

5. Chandra began studying astronomy by asking questions, then answering them. What scientific questions would you like to answer?

CONSTANCE TOM NOGUCHI

Constance Tom Noguchi, Chinese American medical researcher, works in a laboratory. Noguchi believes that traditional Chinese values, such as independent learning and achievement, helped her to become a successful scientist.

When Constance Tom Noguchi (nuh–GOOT–chee) thinks of home, she thinks of books. "We had tremendous numbers of books," she remembers. "I think my father belonged to almost every book club there was." Books arrived almost every day in the mail at the Tom household in San Francisco, California. Many were children's books that James Tom had ordered for his four daughters.

James Tom was a Chinese American engineer who grew up in San Francisco. During World War II he went to work in China. There, he met Irene Cheung (CHUNG), a Chinese citizen. They married, and three of their four daughters were born in China—Connie in 1948. When she was 8 months old, her family moved to San Francisco. (See **Did You Know?** on page 205 for more information on San Francisco's Chinese American population.)

Connie grew up in a home with many reminders of her Chinese heritage. The Toms collected Chinese paintings and sculptures. One of Noguchi's fondest holiday memories is of "the lucky money we received wrapped in red paper. One of my sisters still gives my kids lucky money wrapped in red." Connie and her sisters also learned to speak and write the Chinese language, though they spoke mostly English at home.

The most valuable thing Connie Tom got from her heritage, however, could not be heard or seen. It was intangible.[1] She grew up believing that "self-learning and personal excellence" were very important. Connie learned to ask questions of herself and of the world, and to make decisions on her own.

From her first years in school, Connie liked math and science best. She was enthralled[2] when the teacher brought handfuls of

1. **intangible** (ihn–TAN–juh–buhl) *adj.* not capable of being perceived by the senses
2. **enthralled** (ehn–THRAWLD) *adj.* fascinated

oak leaves to class. The discovery that each of them was different delighted her. How could this be—when they all came from the same tree? Ever the experimenter, Connie grew plants in what she called her "garbage garden." She studied how fast each seed grew, how big each plant became, and how plants differed from one another.

By the time she was in ninth grade, Connie had joined a program for students who liked science. Among the subjects students studied was zoology.[3] The world of animals began to open up for her as the world of plants had earlier. Connie also learned about computers, which would help her later in life.

Students in this program did a lot of investigative[4] work. They may not have known it at the time, but they were using the scientific method. First, they decided on a question and hypothesized[5] what the answer might be. Next, they planned an experiment, based on library research, to test their answer. Then they did the experiment. Finally, they wrote about what had happened and what they had learned. Connie found these experiments "fascinating"—even the planning part, which some people found boring. She also enjoyed making friends who shared her love of science.

Connie was eager to go to college and to study more science. "There was never a question that my sisters and I would go to college. It was just a question of which college," she remembers. She chose the University of California at Berkeley because it was a good school—and her father had gone there.

James Tom was pleased about Connie's interest in science. "He always wanted a doctor, a physician, in the family," she says. Connie liked learning about how animals' bodies worked, so the Toms thought she would become a medical doctor. At Berkeley she took "pre-med" courses, which would prepare her for medical school.

3. **zoology** (zoh-AHL-uh-jee) *n.* the study of animals
4. **investigative** (ihn-VEHS-tuh-gayt-ihv) *adj.* curious; searching into things
5. **hypothesized** (heye-PAHTH-uh-seyezd) *v.* made a theory based on the available facts

While studying pre-med, however, Connie Tom had a change of heart. "It sounds terrible, but I didn't like the attitudes of my classmates," she says. Most of the students who were planning to go to medical school seemed to care more about getting high grades than they did about finding out things for themselves."

Tom found more independence in physics. This branch of science seemed more "personal" to her because most physicists work alone. Also, the physics courses were so hard that students concentrated more on understanding what was being taught than on getting high grades. For this reason, too, the fact that Connie Tom was one of the few women studying physics drew little attention.

Being a woman in a class full of men did cause momentary bewilderment,[6] though. Connie's last name often confused her teachers at first. When they called out "Tom," they thought a man would answer. They were startled when Connie spoke up. "It was something I always laughed at," she says.

While still at Berkeley, Connie Tom met a Japanese American pre-med student named Phil Noguchi. He enjoyed physics as much as Connie did. He also played the guitar and taught Connie to play, too. Connie Tom and Phil Noguchi were married in 1969. Later, they had two sons. Their older son likes to say, "I'm Chinese and Japanese and all American."

Connie Noguchi continued studying physics at George Washington University, in Washington, D.C. But she never stopped wanting to learn about living things. So, Noguchi decided to combine this interest with her knowledge of physics. "When I was in college, the idea of doing research never occurred to me," she says. Now, though, she saw that laboratory research was the "natural" thing to do. In 1975, Noguchi joined the National Institutes of Health in Bethesda, Maryland. This huge medical research center is supported by the U.S. government. Noguchi still works there.

---

6. **bewilderment** (bee-WIHL-duhr-muhnt) *n.* confusion; inability to understand

Noguchi researches diseases of the blood. She has spent years studying sickle cell disease. People with this disease have a problem with a substance called hemoglobin (HEE-moh-gloh-bihn), which carries oxygen through the body. Sickle cell hemoglobin can change the shape of the blood cells that carry it. These cells are supposed to be round like a jelly-filled doughnut. In sickle cell disease, however, some of the cells stretch and curve into a shape that resembles a sickle, a tool once used on farms—and from which the disease gets its name.

At times, the blood of people with sickle cell disease flows slowly. It can become as thick as cream cheese. Blood vessels can become blocked, and cells can die. Children with sickle cell disease do not grow well. They often get colds and are susceptible[7] to infection. In the worst cases, people with sickle cell disease die at an early age.

Today there is no cure for sickle cell disease. Connie Noguchi, however, is looking for treatments that can help victims lead longer and healthier lives. She is studying a drug that increases a "good" form of hemoglobin. If people with sickle cell disease have more of this hemoglobin, more of their cells might behave normally.

Noguchi is also studying the way genes[8] make hemoglobin. Researchers know that the sickle cell gene is inherited from one or both of a victim's parents. They also know that people of African ancestry are more likely than people in other groups to get sickle cell disease. To help them, Noguchi hopes that someday doctors will be able to replace the gene that causes sickle cell disease. Other researchers are also already trying to do this with genes that cause some other diseases.

Although Connie Noguchi is a tireless worker, life is not all peering into a microscope. Her family is very important to her, and she enjoys the richness marrying a man of Japanese descent

7. **susceptible** (suh-SEHP-tuh-buhl) *adj.* easily influenced or affected by

8. **genes** (JEENZ) *n. pl.* chemical units of information found in each cell of the body that are inherited from parents and determine a person's characteristics

has added to her life. They celebrate the holidays and observe some of the customs of both cultures. Noguchi also enjoys helping young people learn about science by inviting them to her laboratory to work with her.

Connie Noguchi feels very fortunate to have found a role in life that suits her so well. As she did as a child, Connie can experiment and learn every day. "It's always fun when things work out the way you expect." But she adds, "It's even more fun when you get unexpected results. . . . That usually causes you to think about the problem in different ways." What is the best thing about a career in science? Noguchi is quick to answer, "getting paid for having fun."

Did You Know? *Almost 80,000 of San Francisco's Chinese Americans live in or near a district called Chinatown. The Toms lived "on the fringe" of Chinatown, and Connie Tom went to school near the heart of this "city within a city." The first people to live there came to the United States in the 1840s from Canton, China, because gold had been discovered in California. They found, though, that there was not enough gold to make their fortune. So, to start a new life, many of the Chinese immigrants worked on the railroad. Later, they worked in the vineyards north of San Francisco. The San Francisco fire of 1906 destroyed Chinatown, but the community quickly rebuilt it. Today, Chinatown is located on some of the most valuable property in San Francisco.*

AFTER YOU READ

EXPLORING YOUR RESPONSES

1. Constance Tom Noguchi's favorite subjects in school were science and math. What are your favorite subjects and why do you like them?

2. Noguchi says that her Chinese heritage helped her value "self-learning and personal excellence." What do "self-learning and personal excellence" mean to you?

3. In ninth grade, Connie Tom joined a program for students who liked science. Which programs or after-school activities might you enjoy? Explain.

4. Noguchi was "turned off" by students who seemed only concerned with getting high grades. What do people miss who are only "after the grade"?

5. Noguchi does research on sickle cell disease. If you could find a cure for a disease, which disease would it be? Why?

UNDERSTANDING WORDS IN CONTEXT

Read the following sentences from the biography. Think about what each underlined word means. In your notebook, write what the word means as it is used in the sentence.

1. The most valuable thing Connie Tom got from her heritage, however, could not be heard or seen. It was intangible.

2. Among the subjects students studied was zoology. The world of animals began to open up for [Connie] as the world of plants had earlier.

3. Students in this program did a lot of . . . work. . . . First, they decided on a question and hypothesized what the answer might be.

4. Being a woman in a class full of men did cause momentary bewilderment, though. . . . When [her teachers] called out "Tom," they thought a man would answer.

5. Children with sickle cell disease do not grow well. They often get colds and are susceptible to infection.

RECALLING DETAILS

1. What did Connie study in her "garbage garden"?

2. Describe the scientific process.

3. Why did Connie Tom switch from pre-med to physics?

4. What kind of research is Noguchi doing now?

5. How has Noguchi's Chinese heritage enriched her life?

UNDERSTANDING INFERENCES

In your notebook, write two or three sentences from the biography that support each of the following inferences.

1. Constance Tom Noguchi likes to work independently.

2. Some research problems take years to investigate.

3. Education is important to Noguchi and her family.

4. Noguchi is concerned with helping others.

5. Grades are just one way of measuring learning.

INTERPRETING WHAT YOU HAVE READ

1. Why might laboratory research have suited Connie Noguchi's need for "self-learning and personal excellence"?

2. In what ways did the science program she joined in ninth grade affect Noguchi?

3. Noguchi's older son says, "I'm Chinese and Japanese and all American." What do you think he means?

4. Why do you think Noguchi has spent years studying one blood disease rather than several problems?

5. Why do you think Noguchi lets high school and college students work with her in the research lab?

ANALYZING QUOTATIONS

Read the following quotation from the biography and answer the questions below.

> *"It's always fun when things work out the way you expect." But she adds, "It's even more fun when you get unexpected results. . . . That usually causes you to think about the problem in different ways."*

1. Why is Noguchi untroubled when her experiments do not turn out the way she thought they would?

2. How is the attitude Noguchi expresses in this quote similar to her attitudes when she was a girl?

3. Why might the unexpected have more power to delight and teach than the expected has?

THINKING CRITICALLY

1. How do you think having so many books available to her affected Connie's future?

2. How do you think having friends in school who also enjoyed science may have helped Noguchi?

3. Noguchi describes her work as "fun." Can a job that takes concentration and produces stress be fun? Explain.

4. How do you think Connie Tom felt about being one of the only women in her physics classes?

5. One reason Noguchi likes her work is that it is like "getting paid for having fun." In what other jobs might a person get paid for having fun? Explain.

SUSUMU TONEGAWA

Susumu Tonegawa, Japanese American biologist, talks to reporters at
his home after winning the 1987 Nobel Prize in medicine. Tonegawa
earned the prize for his research on the body's immune system.

On October 12, 1987, Susumu Tonegawa (soo-SOO-moo toh-neh-GAH-wa) received a telephone call. On the other end of the line was a Japanese reporter. He was calling to congratulate Tonegawa—a Japanese American—for winning the Nobel Prize in medicine. The Nobel Prize is the highest honor a scientist can receive. Tonegawa says, "The first thing I thought was: It must be a mistake."

Far from being a mistake, the prize was well deserved. Tonegawa's research on the body's immune system[1] was the reason for the award. As David Baltimore, a medical researcher, has said, "It can't be overestimated how important [Tonegawa's] revelation[2] was." As described by author Joel Davis, this revelation had to do with how the immune system is able to "defend the body against nearly everything the universe can throw at it."

Previously, scientists had wondered how the immune system recognizes and responds to the millions of different disease-causing germs that enter the body. Scientists did know that each individual germ has to be fought off by the immune system. The immune system must then "remember" the germ so that the next time it enters the body, it will be destroyed. What scientists could not understand was how the immune system's basic building blocks, or cells,[3] could handle this huge job. Each cell has thousands of genes,[4] which carry the instructions for making the chemicals that the body needs. Yet the numbers just did not seem to add up.

---

1. **immune system** (ihm-YOON SIHS-tuhm) a complex network of cells and chemicals that helps the body fight disease

2. **revelation** (rehv-uh-LAY-shuhn) *n.* an astonishing find

3. **cells** (SEHLZ) *n. pl.* the tiny living units of which all living things are made

4. **genes** (JEENZ) *n. pl.* substances in cells that give the body instructions about a person's traits and chemical make-up

In the late 1970s, Tonegawa found that the instructions for each antibody[5] come from a number of different genes. He proved that because many genes are involved, they can "mix and match" to make instructions for all of the necessary antibodies. As Tonegawa says, "It's like when GM [General Motors] builds a car that they want to meet the . . . needs of many customers. If they custom-make each car, it is not economical. So they make different parts, then they assemble it in different ways. . . . Therefore, one can make different cars. It's a matter of how you assemble those pieces."

Tonegawa also found that genes are not permanently in place; they can move around as a body grows and develops. For example, he showed that some genes with information about antibodies were far away from each other in the cells of mice embryos.[6] By the time the mice became adults, however, the genes had "shuffled" to different places. Tonegawa says that this moving is like changing the order of boxcars on a freight train. Scientists had thought that the order of the genes in a living thing could not be changed. In other words, "the freight train never shifts its cars around." Tonegawa showed that the cars on the train can shift.

Susumu was born in Nagoya (nuh–GOY-uh), Japan, on September 5, 1939. He grew up in Japan and received his schooling there, graduating from Kyoto (kee–OHT-oh) University in 1963. (See **Did You Know?** on page 213 for more information on Japanese schools.) He then came to the United States to continue his studies in science. He received his Ph.D. from the University of California at San Diego in 1968. Then he stayed in San Diego to work at the famous Salk Institute, a laboratory for medical research.

----

5. **antibody** (ANT-ih-bah-dee) *n.* a chemical produced by the body to try to fight off disease

6. **embryos** (EHM-bree-ohz) *n. pl.* animals in very early states of development, before birth

When Tonegawa's U.S. visa[7] expired in 1971, he went to work at a laboratory in Basel, Switzerland. There he completed much of the work that later would win him the Nobel Prize.

Changing scientists' views about genes was not easy. Tonegawa worked for years, but even when his experiments began to show the results he wanted, he did not dare to believe it at first. "I still remember the day I went to the lab and saw the results," he says. "I was very glad to see the experiment worked. But it took not even days—but months—to realize what the impact of this was. I guess these things take time."

In 1981, Susumu returned to the United States. He joined the Massachusetts Institute of Technology (M.I.T.), where he still works at the Center for Cancer Research. Tonegawa's findings about genes and antibodies have proven to be very useful in the search for knowledge about cancer. Watching the movement of genes, for example, has led to explanations of how certain kinds of cancers are formed.

Susumu Tonegawa often stays in his laboratory until late at night to finish an experiment. Nancy Hopkins, a teacher at M.I.T., says, "Susumu is really a spectacular scientist. . . . He's the kind of person who moves by insight.[8] . . . There is a force in him, and when he has it, you feel it too."

Tonegawa's wife, Mayumi (meye-YOO-mee), has described another important side of him. "He doesn't have any prejudices[9] before he begins work," she said. Tonegawa's open mind is one explanation for his success. Mayumi also points out that Tonegawa is "much more interested in what he's doing rather than what he has done."

This pride is echoed by Susumu's father, who was one of the first people to call him after the Nobel Prize was announced.

---

7. **visa** (VEE-zuh) *n.* official papers that allow a person to enter or live in a foreign country

8. **insight** (IHN-seyet) *n.* the ability to understand the inner nature of things

9. **prejudices** (PREHJ-uh-dihs-uhz) *n. pl.* judgments or ideas formed before the facts are known

"He may be even more glad than I" about the prize, Susumu later told reporters. "He always felt I would win, but he always wondered whether I would win while he was alive."

As important as Tonegawa's findings have been, he remains a "down-to-earth" person. "It took several days to realize how thrilling [winning the Nobel Prize] is," he said. "It came on very slowly. When other people win, you feel they are high up and so special. But when you win, you think they're not that special. They're just normal people." Susumu also expresses surprise that several other scientists were not honored at the same time he was. "You can't do this kind of work by yourself," Tonegawa emphasizes. He feels that the findings of other scientists were helpful to him in making his discoveries.

Susumu also has one other way of keeping his achievements in perspective.[10] When asked how important winning the Nobel Prize was, Susumu looked at Hidde (HIH–day), his 9-month-old son. "The birth of my son is greater than this," he said.

> **Did You Know?** *The modern Japanese education system has had many influences. At the beginning of the 1900s, it was modeled on the German system. All students attended school for six years. The course of study, however, was centered on ancient Japanese religious beliefs and morals. After World War II, Japanese education was influenced by the U.S. system. Courses centered on giving students practical knowledge rather than rules for living. Schooling has become so important in the Japanese culture that nearly all school-aged children attend. Competition to enter universities is very intense because many Japanese believe that the school they attend determines how successful they will be throughout their careers.*

---

10. **perspective** (puhr-SPEHK-tihv) *n.* a point of view that shows things in their true relationship to one another

AFTER YOU READ

EXPLORING YOUR RESPONSES

1. Many scientists think the Nobel Prize is the highest honor they can win. What prize or award would you most like to win? Why?

2. Think of a career that interests you. Name five qualities you think would help someone do well in that field. Explain your choices.

3. Tonegawa wanted to solve a mystery about the immune system. What mystery would you like to solve? Why?

4. Tonegawa studied and worked in three different countries. What do you think are the good and bad points of living and working in several different countries?

5. Tonegawa said of his research, "You can't do this kind of work by yourself." Tell about a time when you have benefited from the work of others.

UNDERSTANDING WORDS IN CONTEXT

Read the following sentences from the biography. Think about what each underlined word means. In your notebook, write what the word means as it is used in the sentence.

1. Tonegawa's research on the body's immune system . . . had to do with how the immune system is able to "defend the body against nearly everything the universe can throw at it."

2. What scientists could not understand was how the immune system's basic building blocks, or cells, could handle this huge job.

3. Each cell has thousands of genes, which carry the instructions for making the chemicals that the body needs.

4. Susumu also has one other way of keeping his achievements in perspective. When asked how important the Nobel Prize was, Susumu looked at . . . his 9-month-old son. "The birth of my son is greater than this," he said.

5. "He doesn't have any prejudices before he begins work," [Mayumi] said after her husband won the Nobel Prize. Tonegawa's open mind in his research is one explanation for his success.

RECALLING DETAILS

1. What two important facts did Susumu Tonegawa uncover about genes?

2. How did Tonegawa react when he learned he had won the Nobel Prize?

3. Why did Susumu leave the United States in 1971?

4. Where does Tonegawa work today?

5. How did Susumu's father react to the news about the Nobel Prize?

UNDERSTANDING INFERENCES

In your notebook, write two or three sentences from the biography that support each of the following inferences.

1. Susumu Tonegawa had not expected to win the Nobel Prize.

2. Tonegawa's father was proud of his son's work.

3. Genes can change in more ways than scientists once thought they could.

4. Patience and hard work were important to Tonegawa's success.

5. Family life is very important to Tonegawa.

INTERPRETING WHAT YOU HAVE READ

1. Why are research scientists like Tonegawa as important to the field of medicine as doctors are?

2. Antibodies stay in the blood after disease-causing germs are destroyed. How does this help the body?

3. Why does the Nobel Prize committee often give awards to several people instead of just one individual?

4. Why would Tonegawa choose to describe his ideas in terms of everyday items, such as boxcars?

5. Which personal quality do you think is most important to Tonegawa's success?

ANALYZING QUOTATIONS

Read the following quotation from the biography and answer the questions below.

> "I still remember the day I went to the lab and saw the results. I was very glad to see the experiment worked. But it took not even days—but months—to realize what the impact of this was. I guess these things take time."

1. What does this quotation reveal about Tonegawa's personality?

2. What was the impact of Tonegawa's findings?

3. How do you respond to unexpected good news?

THINKING CRITICALLY

1. Another teacher at M.I.T. says, "Susumu . . . moves by insight." How might insight be useful in scientific research?

2. Based on this biography, name three qualities of work that can win a Nobel Prize.

3. Susumu's wife once said about him, "He's much more interested in what he's doing rather than what he has done." How does the biography support this statement?

4. Why are well-known ideas sometimes difficult to change?

5. Why do you think Tonegawa's findings were so important in finding ways to cure disease?

JUAN MONTERO

Juan Montero (left), Filipino American surgeon, accepts a
Community Service Award. With this award, the Medical Society
of Virginia honors Montero's commitment to improving the health
of the poor.

The operating room seemed a million miles from the auditorium where Dr. Juan Montero (HWAWN mohn-TER-oh) and his wife Meri were watching the Filipino (fihl-ih-PEE-noh) dancers. Suddenly, Montero's beeper sounded. A family had been involved in a car accident. The doctor rushed to the emergency room of the hospital.

Most of the injuries were minor. The 12-year-old boy, whose pelvis[1] had been crushed, seemed to be recovering nicely. His blood pressure and other vital signs[2] were stabilizing.[3] Dr. Montero checked for bleeding, but found none.

About three days later, however, the boy started bleeding inside his stomach and intestine. He was losing blood as fast as the doctors could replace it.

The boy was too weak for another operation, so Montero began trying every drug that he thought might help. But the boy continued to bleed. Then Montero began searching his notebooks, where he found a note about a drug called Pitressin (pih-TREHS-ihn). This drug was used mainly in childbirth. However, some doctors were using it to stop bleeding in the stomach and intestine.

Dr. Montero knew that using Pitressin was risky—but there was nothing left to try. So, he took the chance. As the drug started to seep into his body, the boy's face turned as white as a piece of paper. He clutched his chest, screaming with pain. But the bleeding began to slow down. Finally, it stopped.

---

1. **pelvis** (PEHL-vihs) *n.* a basin-shaped bone that supports the middle part of the body

2. **vital signs** measurements of the activity of the vital organs, such as the heart, brain, and lungs

3. **stabilizing** (STAY-buh-leyez-ihng) *v.* showing less change; becoming normal

Five years later, in 1979, Doctor Montero was watching the boy whose life he had saved graduate from high school as class valedictorian.[4] The boy, who had almost died, would go on to study medicine himself. Montero marvels[5] at the role "luck" plays in his profession: "It was hard to believe that with a flickering memory of one medicine, you could bring back a life almost lost. It never ceases to amaze me what [a] thin line separates life from death—often as thin as the mark of a knife blade."

Juan Montero was born in the Philippine islands in 1942. At that time, World War II was being fought, and Japanese armies were invading the islands. The Montero family and many others fled into the hills, traveling incognito[6] to escape discovery. Juan, who was just a toddler, made the journey from place to place on his grandmother's back.

After the war, the Monteros settled in a little town called Bayabas (bah-YAH-bahs). Despite the hardships of war and of starting a new life, many of Montero's memories of his early childhood are happy ones.

At first, Juan hated school. However, he soon realized that he had an excellent memory, and began to like learning. Like most Filipinos, Juan was taught both his native language, Tagalog (tah-GAH-lahg), and English in school. (See **Did You Know?** on page 222 for more information on Tagalog.) In fact, most of his books were in English, but Juan had little trouble learning this foreign language.

Juan went away to high school in Cebu (SAY-boo) City, in the southern Philippines. Juan graduated when he was not quite 16. That summer, he began to take pre-med college courses. Juan had no doubts about his future career. "My parents kept telling me from the very beginning of my schooling that I was going to be a doctor. I did not argue then nor ever."

---

4. **valedictorian** (val-uh-dihk-TOHR-ee-ahn) *n.* a student, usually the top student in the class, chosen to give a speech at graduation

5. **marvels** (MAHR-vuhlz) *v.* regards with wonder or surprise

6. **incognito** (ihn-kahg-NEE-toh) *adv.* in disguise

In 1960, Montero went to medical school at Velez (veh–LEZ) Hospital. "I couldn't help but be apprehensive[7] about one awesome thought," Montero recalls, "that it would no longer be cats and dogs that we'd deal with, but the human body." Apprehensive or not, he did very well–and he even found time to be elected president of the Medical Student Council. He also helped start a program to care for poor people in the countryside, where he and other students drove around in a "hospital on wheels."

Montero's work among the poor helped him decide to specialize in surgery, the branch of medicine that involves repairing or removing diseased or damaged parts of the body. To him, surgery seemed especially challenging and rewarding. A successful operation requires perfect teamwork–something Montero values highly.

At the same time, the operating surgeon must accept final responsibility for what happens to the patient. Montero explains, "So I always thought of it as here is a patient whose life is at stake. It depends on what I do! I have to do my very best. . . . Attention must be paid to every detail."

New doctors usually work as interns,[8] learning from more experienced doctors, to complete their education. Montero came to the United States for his internship–first to Norfolk, Virginia, then to the University of Virginia in Charlottesville. He learned about new ways of doing surgery and practiced the skills he would need to save lives. He also met his future wife, Mary, nicknamed Meri, Goodsell. They were married in 1970. "Meri is a real 'melting pot' American," Montero notes. "She is of English, German, Scotch Irish, and Dutch descent. . . . Add all this with my history and one can see why our children are true internationals, a marvelous combination."

---

7. **apprehensive** (ap-ree-HEHN-sihv) *adj.* anxious or fearful about the future

8. **interns** (IHN-ternz) *n. pl.* recently graduated doctors who are working with more experienced doctors in a hospital

In 1972, the new doctor soon got a lucky break. William Hotchkiss, an expert in chest surgery, offered to share his office in Norfolk with Montero. He had seen Montero's surgical work and admired it. Montero told Dr. Hotchkiss that he had decided to stay in the United States rather than return to the Philippines, where political unrest was rapidly growing. He welcomed the future—a new wife, a new home, and a promising career.

Like most careers, though, it had its bumps—and its lessons. In 1973, Montero operated successfully on a man whose abdomen had been badly torn in an accident. He and his team felt very happy to have saved someone who "was lucky to [have reached] the hospital alive." Two days later, however, the man died. Montero thoroughly reviewed the operation and concluded that he had done his best. Montero was learning that as a surgeon he could not work miracles. This knowledge gave him great confidence to continue.

But this confidence was soon shaken. To become a fully certified[9] surgeon, Montero would have to pass two tests given by the American Board of Surgery. Montero passed the written part of the test without difficulty. The oral examination, however, was another matter. In this part of the test, examiners ask difficult questions that have to be answered out loud quickly and completely. Montero failed the oral exam twice. Montero recalls, "this was the most stern test of my inner self."

Determined not to fail again, Juan Montero took two special courses in surgery. He also read many papers, and two doctor friends helped him practice a "dry run" of the oral exam. Finally, in 1976, Montero passed the oral test.

In the late 1970s and early 1980s, Montero was busy not only with his practice but also with community work, such as setting up clinics on the Virginia coast for poor farm workers. Then, in 1982, Montero's wish to use his surgical skill to help his people came true. He, along with other Filipino American doctors,

---

9. **certified** (SERT-uh-feyed) *adj.* having passed a test and earned a certificate

went back to the Philippines, where there was a tremendous need for medical care. This team performed dozens of operations, day after day, often under very difficult conditions. It was Montero's way of honoring his rich heritage.

Also in 1982, Montero published his autobiography, *Halfway Through*. In it, he describes the first 35 years of a life that "contained anything but boredom." True to his belief in helping others, he dedicates the book to "the less fortunate, ambitious youths of the world—conscious that every beginning is hard." Juan Montero knows a lot about hard beginnings, but he knows a lot about the courage to overcome obstacles, too. As Montero says, the important thing is to "do your best."

> **Did You Know?** *Tagalog is one of the native languages spoken in the Philippines, a diverse country that is made up of more than 7,000 islands. Tagalog is spoken by the people of the island of Luzon (loo-ZAHN), which includes the capital city of Manila. Because it is the native language of many people in the capital city, speakers of Tagalog have many important positions in manufacturing, business, and the professions. Tagalog is also the basis of Pilipino (pihl-uh-PEE-noh), one of the official national language of the Philippines. The country's other official language is English. Of a population of about 62 million Filipinos, 12 million speak Tagalog, 30 million speak Pilipino, and 47 million speak English.*

AFTER YOU READ

EXPLORING YOUR RESPONSES

1. Juan Montero has many happy memories of growing up in the Philippines, even though his family faced many hardships. Why might it be important to "see beyond" the bad things that happen in life?

2. Being a surgeon requires making "life and death" decisions under great pressure. What qualities do you think would help a person become a good surgeon?

3. Montero had to go to school many years to become a surgeon. Why do you think becoming a surgeon requires so much education?

4. Surgical operations require teamwork. Which tasks are better accomplished by a team than by an individual?

5. Montero felt great confidence when he realized that he had done his best—even though the patient died. How might you have felt if you were in his place?

UNDERSTANDING WORDS IN CONTEXT

Read the following sentences from the biography. Think about what each underlined word means. In your notebook, write what the word means as it is used in the sentence.

1. The 12-year-old boy, whose pelvis had been crushed, seemed to be recovering nicely. His blood pressure and other vital signs were stabilizing.

2. Montero marvels at the role "luck" plays in his profession: "It was hard to believe that with a flickering memory of one medicine, you could bring back a life almost lost."

3. The Montero family and many others fled into the hills, traveling incognito to escape discovery.

4. "I couldn't help but be <u>apprehensive</u> about one awesome thought," Montero recalls, "that it would no longer be cats and dogs that we'd deal with [as surgeons], but the human body."

5. New doctors usually work as <u>interns</u>, learning from more experienced doctors, to complete their education.

RECALLING DETAILS

1. How did Dr. Montero finally stop the bleeding of the 12-year-old boy?

2. Whose idea was it for Montero to become a doctor?

3. What caused the trouble in the Philippines when Juan was very young?

4. Describe a surgeon's work.

5. What did Montero do when he failed the oral exam for surgery?

UNDERSTANDING INFERENCES

In your notebook, write two or three sentences from the biography that support each of the following inferences.

1. Montero works well with others.

2. Becoming a surgeon requires many years of hard work.

3. Children can be influenced by adults in many ways.

4. Juan Montero cares about others.

5. Sometimes failure teaches people more than success does.

INTERPRETING WHAT YOU HAVE READ

1. Why did Montero use Pitressin on the boy who had been in the car accident even though he knew using the drug was risky?

2. Why do you think Montero chose to be a surgeon?

3. As a surgeon, how was Montero able to put his good memory to use?

4. Why might Montero consider failing the oral exam "the most stern test of my inner self"?

5. How was Montero able to use his medical skills to help Filipinos?

ANALYZING QUOTATIONS

Read the following quotation from the biography and answer the questions below.

> *"It never ceases to amaze me what [a] thin line separates life from death–often as thin as the mark of a knife blade.*

1. What do you think Montero means by saying "a thin line separates life from death"?

2. Why do you think Montero chose "the mark of a knife blade" to describe the "thin line" that "separates life from death"?

3. Think about a life and death situation you have read about or seen on TV or in the movies. In that situation, what made the difference between the person's living and dying?

THINKING CRITICALLY

1. Why do you think saving the life of the 12-year-old boy meant so much to Montero?

2. Montero "hated school" at first. What do you think made him change his mind about school and learning?

3. How might Montero's life have been different if he had decided to return to the Philippines instead of staying in the United States?

4. Montero has learned not to feel guilty if he has done his best but the patient dies. Why do you think it is important for a surgeon to learn this lesson?

5. Montero says, "One thing I've learned is that whatever you do best in life, do your best at it. Chances are you will come out ahead." Think of something you do well. What would it mean to do your best at it?

CULTURAL CONNECTIONS

Thinking About What People Do

1. Imagine that you are president of an organization that is giving an award to one of the people in this unit. Write the speech you will give as you present the award. Tell why your group is making the award and why this person deserves it. Present your speech to the class.

2. Imagine you are one of the people in this unit. Write three journal entries describing "your" experiences and thoughts on three different days. Include details about "your" work.

3. Create a poster encouraging young people to go into one of the fields described in this unit. Use information from the biographies to make your poster educational. Present your poster to the class.

Thinking About Culture

1. How did the cultural backgrounds of the subjects in this unit affect their choice of career? Choose one person and use details from his or her biography to support your conclusions.

2. Compare the educational backgrounds of two people from this unit. What effects did culture have on their education?

3. Imagine that you are one of the people in this unit. Write a letter to a group of children, teaching them something about "your" culture. Base your letter on the facts from the person's biography.

Building Research Skills

Work with a partner to complete the following activity.

Find out more about one of the careers or fields discussed in this unit. You may wish to select a career that you are considering for your future.

> **Hint:** The Bibliography at the back of this book will give you ideas about articles and books to help you start your research.

Schedule an interview with someone in your community who works in that field. Make a list of questions you have about the work he or she does. You might ask the following questions:

> **Hint:** To gather more information about this field, you might talk to a guidance counselor at your school.

☆ What does a person in this field actually do in a typical day?

☆ Where are the jobs in this field?

☆ What are the salary ranges for jobs in this field?

☆ What classes would a person take in high school or college to prepare for this field?

☆ Is further education needed?

☆ Where could I write for more information about this field?

> **Hint:** Before you record an interview, discuss with the interviewee why the tape will be helpful to you. Make sure that he or she is willing to have the conversation recorded.

Go to the library to learn more about your chosen career. As you conduct your research, you may find additional questions you wish to ask your interviewee.

Next, conduct the interview. If the interviewee consents, you may wish to tape-record the interview. Take notes, too, to help you stay on track and to protect against tape failure.

Share the findings from your interview in the form of an oral presentation. You may wish to play part of the tape as part of your report.

Extending Your Studies

SOCIAL STUDIES **Your task:** *To make a Venn diagram that shows the similarities and differences between the United States Senate and the House of Representatives.*
You read that Patsy Takemoto Mink is a member of the U.S. House of Representatives, which is one of the legislative branches of Congress. The other branch is the U.S. Senate.

Look for information on Congress in your social studies book or in the library. Then fill in a Venn diagram like the one shown below with information on how the Senate and the House of Representatives are alike and how they are different. Include categories such as number of members, lengths of terms, roles in making a bill into law, and types of subcommittees.

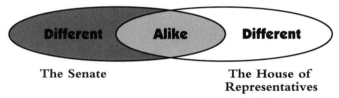

| Different | Alike | Different |
| The Senate | | The House of Representatives |

Have a class discussion on the similarities and differences between the Senate and House, then display your Venn diagrams on your bulletin board.

MATH **Your task:** *To use an abacus to show numbers.*
Thousands of years ago, people in China and Japan developed a type of calculator called an *abacus.* There are two kinds of abacuses—the rod abacus and the bead abacus, both of which are still used today for mathematical calculations.

Each of the bead abacuses below shows the same number, 683. Work with a partner to figure out how one of the abacuses shows that number. Then, on a piece of paper, draw a picture of that abacus showing the number 1,692. Compare your abacus with that of another pair of students.

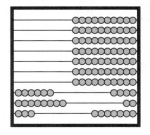 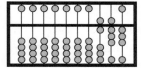 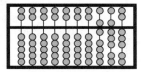

 **HEALTH** **Your task:** *To persuade an audience that all children should, or should not, receive immunizations paid for by the Federal government.* In reading Susumu Tonegawa's biography, you learned some facts about the body's immune system. Vaccines help the immune system resist serious diseases such as polio, whooping cough, and German measles. When you receive a vaccine, you are actually being exposed to the germ that causes a disease, but the germ has been weakened so that you will not actually get the disease. Your body will, however, produce antibodies that fight the germ. In this way, you become immune to the disease.

Call your doctor or a local health clinic, or go to the library to research how vaccines are used in the United States today. You might begin with these questions:

☆ What percentage of children in the United States receives vaccines?

☆ How much do the vaccines cost?

☆ How dangerous are the diseases that vaccines help prevent?

☆ What is the cost of treating the diseases?

☆ Do children of all income levels receive vaccines?

Write a persuasive paragraph, or make an oral presentation to your class, telling why you think all children should or should not receive immunizations paid for by the Federal government.

WRITING WORKSHOP

In Units 2 and 3, you wrote biographical sketches of a friend and of a family or community member. The information for these sketches came from your memory or from interviews. For this sketch, you will use books, magazines, and other sources to write a **researched biography**.

PREWRITING

Select a subject:　Jot down the names of three or four people whose work or life appeals to you. Next to each name write two phrases that describe this person. Then choose the person who interests you most.

Locate and collect materials:　Use the card catalog in your library to locate books on your subject. Look for your subject's last name and note the titles you find and their call numbers. For example:

Author	Title	Call Number
Momaday, N. Scott	*Ancestral Voice*	813.54 M739

The librarian can help you locate the materials and suggest other sources. The *Readers' Guide to Periodical Literature* will help you find magazine articles. If you write about one of the subjects in this book, check the Bibliography on pages 244–247 for resources.

Gather information:　Once you find materials, think of questions about your subject. Write each question at the top of a note card. For example:

☆ What were some important events in the person's life?

☆ What dreams or ambitions did the person have?

☆ What has the person accomplished?

☆ What has the person said that is interesting?

☆ What makes the person's life noteworthy?

When you find a fact that answers a question, write it on the appropriate note card. Create new cards as needed.

Find your focus: When you finish taking notes, reread your note cards. What idea connects the events of this person's life? For example, let us say that your subject is a doctor who once cared for the wealthy, but is now helping the poor instead. Focus on what caused this person to turn from fame and fortune to helping less fortunate people. Select two or three events that illustrate this idea.

DRAFTING

In your notebook, write your subject's name, your main idea, and the events you will write about. For example:

Subject: Dr. Alberta Grace
Main Idea: Dr. Grace learns that helping people is more rewarding than money and fame.
Event 1: Grace finds herself in her old neighborhood where she sees many homeless people and children who are hungry and do not have medical care.
Event 2: Grace leaves her uptown clinic and sets up a practice in her old neighborhood.

The Opening: The opening should introduce your subject and focus and hold your reader's attention. For example:

> *When Alberta Grace was a student at Harvard Medical School, she dreamed of having a big house and a fancy car. However, midway through her career, Grace changed her mind about what it means to be a successful doctor.*

The Body: Here you will bring your subject to life through your details. Direct quotes from the subject are especially revealing.

The Closing: By the end of the biography, your reader should be able to "see" your subject and understand your main idea. In our example, the idea was that helping people is more rewarding than money and fame.

> *"When people have so little, anything you give becomes great," Dr. Grace says. One thing she has brought her community is hope. For more than ten years, Dr. Alberta Grace has been dispensing medicine, and hope.*

Include a bibliography: At the end of your biography, list, in alphabetical order, the materials you have used. Use this form:

Books:

Author	Title	City Published	Publisher	Copyright Date
Smith, Charles.	Alberta Grace.	New York:	Overland Press,	1992.

Magazines:

Author	Article Title	Magazine Title	Date	Page Numbers
Field, Renee.	"Dispensing Hope."	Lives Today.	30 April 1991:	55–57.

REVISING

Put your biography aside for a day or two. Then, with the help of another student who will act as your editor, evaluate and revise your work. See the directions for writers and student editors below.

Directions for Writers: Before giving your biography to your student editor, ask yourself these questions:

☆ Does the opening grab the reader's attention?

☆ Am I *showing*, not *telling*, the reader what happened?

☆ Are the ideas presented in logical order?

☆ Have I included quotes?

☆ Does the ending sum up the main idea and leave the reader with a lasting impression?

Make notes for your next draft or revise your work before you give it to your student editor. Then ask your editor to read your work. Listen carefully to his or her suggestions. If they seem helpful, use them to improve your writing when you revise your work.

Directions for Student Editors: Read the work carefully and respectfully, remembering that your purpose is to help the writer do his or her best work. Keep in mind that an editor should always make positive, helpful comments that point to specific parts of the essay. After you read the work, use these questions to help direct your comments:

☆ What do I like most about the biography?

☆ Do I feel that I know the subject?

☆ Has the writer used details to describe the subject?

☆ Are these details organized clearly?

☆ What would I like to know more about?

PROOFREADING

When you are satisfied that your work says what you want it to say, check it carefully for errors in spelling, punctuation, grammar, and capitalization. Then, make a neat, final copy of your work.

PUBLISHING

After you revise your biography, you are ready to publish it. Present your work to the class, showing your sources and pictures of your subject, if possible.

GLOSSARY

PRONUNCIATION KEY

Vowel Sound	Symbol	Respelling
a as in *hat*	a	HAT
a as in *day, date, paid*	ay	DAY, DAYT, PAYD
vowels as in *far, on*	ah	FAHR, AHN
vowels as in *dare, air*	ai	DAIR, AIR
vowels as in *saw, call, pour*	aw	SAW, KAWL, PAWR
e as in *pet, debt*	eh	PEHT, DEHT
e as in *seat, chief;* **y** as in *beauty*	ee	SEET, CHEEF, BYOO-tee
vowels as in *learn, fur, sir*	er	LERN, FER, SER
i as in *sit, bitter;* **ee** as in *been*	ih	SIHT, BIHT-uhr, BIHN
i as in *mile;* **y** as in *defy;*	eye	MEYEL, dee-FEYE,
ei as in *height;*	eye	HEYET
o as in *go*	oh	GOH
vowels as in *boil, toy*	oi	BOIL, TOI
vowels as in *foot, could*	oŏ	FOOT, KOOD
vowels as in *boot, rule, suit*	oo	BOOT, ROOL, SOOT
vowels as in *how, out, bough*	ow	HOW, OWT, BOW
vowels as in *up, come*	u	UP, KUM
vowels as in *use, use, few*	yoo	YOOZ, YOOS, FYOO
vowels in unaccented syllables (schwas) *again, upon, sanity*	uh	uh-GEHN, uh-PAHN, SAN-uh-tee

Consonant Sound	Symbol	Respelling
ch as in *choose, reach*	ch	CHOOZ, REECH
g as in *go, dig*	g	GOH, DIHG
j as in *jar;* **dg** as in *fudge;* **g** as in *gem*	j	JAHR, FUJ, JEHM
k as in *king;* **c** as in *come;* **ch** as in *Christmas*	k	KIHNG, KUM, KRIHS-muhs
s as in *treasure;* **g** as in *bourgeois*	zh	TREH-zhuhr, boor-ZHWAH
sh as in *ship*	sh	SHIHP
th as in *thin*	th	THIHN
th as in *this*	th	THIHS
z as in *zero;* **s** as in *chasm*	z	ZEE-roh, KAZ-uhm
x as in *fix, axle*	ks	FIHKS, AK-suhl
x as in *exist*	gz	ihg-ZIHST
s as in *this, sir*	s	THIS, SER
wh as in *white*	wh	WHEYET
h as in *who, whole*	h	HOO, HOHL
gh as in *rough, laugh*	f	RUF, LAF
ph as in *telephone*	f	TEHL-uh-fohn

absurd (ab-SERD) *adj.* clearly wrong or unreasonable; very silly, 195

ambassador (am-BAS-uh-duhr) *n.* a special representative, 84

anguish (ANG-gwihsh) *n.* great suffering and agony, 120

antibody (ANT-ih-bah-dee) *n.* a chemical produced by the body to try to fight off disease, 211

apply (uh-PLEYE) *v.* to put to some practical use, 176

apprehensive (ap-ree-HEHN-sihv) *adj.* anxious or fearful about the future, 220

aptitude (AP-tuh-tood) *n.* a natural ability or talent, 128

archaeologist (ahr-kee-AHL-uh-jihst) *n.* a person who studies past civilizations, 38

architect (AHR-kuh-tehkt) *n.* a person whose profession is designing buildings, bridges, or other structures, 72, 100

artistry (AHRT-ihs-tree) *n.* artistic ability or work, 139

aspiring (uh-speyer-ihng) *adj.* reaching for a high goal, 101

assimilate (uh-SIHM-uh-layt) *v.* to absorb groups of different cultures into the main culture, 7

astronomy (uh-STRAHN-uh-mee) *n.* the study of stars and planets, 193

auditioned (aw-DIHSH-uhnd) *v.* performed or acted at a tryout, 122

baton (buh-TAHN) *n.* a stick used by the conductor to guide an orchestra, 156

bewilderment (bee-WIHL-duhr-muhnt) *n.* confusion; inability to understand, 203

calligraphy (kuh-LIHG-ruh-fee) *n.* beautiful, artistic handwriting, 86

campaign (kam-PAYN) *n.* a series of connected battles in a war, 64

casting director the person who chooses the actors for parts in movies, TV programs, and plays, 150

celebrity (suh-LEHB-ruh-tee) *n.* wide recognition; fame, 132

cello (CHEHL-oh) *n.* a stringed musical instrument that is larger than a violin and makes a lower sound, 157

cells (SEHLZ) *n. pl.* the tiny living units of which all living things are made, 210

certified (SERT-uh-feyed) *adj.* having passed a test and earned a certificate, 221

chaos (KAY-ahs) *n.* a state of total confusion, 147

civil rights (SIHV-uhl REYETS) *n. pl.* rights guaranteed by the U.S. Constitution and other acts of Congress, 75

cliff dwellings apartments with many stories that were built about a thousand years ago under overhanging cliffs by Native Americans in what is now the southwestern United States, 103

collaborated (kuh-LAB-u-ray-tihd) *v.* worked together, 85

competitive (kuhm-PEHT-uh-tihv) *adj.* trying to win a contest, 138

compromised (KAHM-pruh-meyezd) *v.* reached a solution that considers both sides of an issue, 194

conductor (kuhn-DUK-tuhr) *n.* the person who leads an orchestra, 156

conscience (KAHN-shuhnts) *n.* a knowledge or sense of right and wrong, with an urge to do right, 75

conservative (kuhn-SER-vuh-tihv) *adj.* cautious; safe, 140

consistency (kuhn-SIHS-tuhn-see) *n.* agreement with what has already been done or expressed, 141

conviction (kuhn-VIHK-shuhn) *n.* strong belief, 130

correspondent (kawr-uh-SPAHN-duhnt) *n.* a person who makes regular reports to a newspaper, magazine, or broadcast network, 150

deadlines (DEHD-leyenz) *n. pl.* the times by which things must be done, 94

debut (day-BYOO) *n.* the first formal appearance, 131

dedicated (DEHD-ih-kayt-uhd) *v.* opened formally to the public, 74

defect (dee-FEKT) *v.* to leave one's country and join with another country that is opposed to the first one, 120

depressed (dee-PREHST) *adj.* feeling gloomy or sad, 158

dictator (DIHK-tayt-uhr) *n.* a ruler with complete power, 147

differentiate (dihf-uhr-EHN-shee-ayt) *v.* to see differences between things, 26

diligence (DIHL-uh-juhns) *n.* constant effort, 122

diploma (dih-PLOH-muh) *n.* a document saying that someone has graduated from a school or college, 44

diplomat (DIHP-luh-mat) *n.* a person who handles negotiations between nations, 91

dismayed (dihs-MAYD) *adj.* suddenly disappointed or frightened, 36

dissenters (dih-SEHNT-uhrz) *n. pl.* people who disagree with a belief, idea, or policy; protesters, 187

drudgery (DRUJ-uhr-ee) *n.* work that is hard and boring, 178

dual (DOO-uhl) *adj.* having two parts, 159

elements (EHL-uh-muhnts) *n. pl.* parts; specific patterns or movements, 140

embassy (EHM-buh-see) *n.* the office of the representatives of a foreign country, 91

embryos (EHM-bree-ohz) *n. pl.* animals in very early states of development, before birth, 211

emigrated (EHM-uh-grayt-uhd) *v.* left one country or region to settle in another, 7

enthralled (ehn-THRAWLD) *adj.* fascinated, 201

entrepreneur (ahn-truh-pruh-NER) *n.* a person who takes risks in starting a new business, 178

equations (ee-KWAY-zhuhnz) *n. pl.* mathematical statements that describe an event or thing with numbers, 195

erupted (ee-RUHPT-ihd) *v.* broke out or burst forth, 176

essence (EHS-uhns) *n.* the most important or basic quality of something, 187

evacuate (ee-VAK-yoo-ayt) *v.* to remove, 120

exile (EHKS-eyel) *n.* a person forced to leave his or her homeland, 16

exploit (ehks-PLOIT) *v.* to use or take advantage of something, 37

faltering (FAWL-tuhr-ihng) *v.* moving in a hesitating, unsteady way, 34

FBI (Federal Bureau of Investigation) a government agency that investigates crimes against the United States, 43

fellowship (FEHL-oh-shihp) *n.* a gift of money that pays for a graduate student's or scholar's studies, 45

fiction (FIHK-shuhn) *n.* a story that is invented or made up rather than true life, 46

flourish (FLER-ihsh) *v.* grow and prosper, 83

freelance (FREE-lans) *adj.* independent, working on a project basis, 84

full-fledged (FOOL FLEHJD) *adj.* complete; completely developed, 43

fusion (FYOO-zhun) *n.* a union of two things, 67

genes (JEENZ) *n. pl.* chemical units of information found in each cell of the body that are inherited from parents and determine a person's characteristics, 204, 210

geologist (jee-AHL-uh-jihst) *n.* a scientist who studies rocks and minerals to learn about the earth, 185

grant (GRANT) *n.* a gift of money to be used to work on a project, 45

guide wires wires that visually impaired people can grasp and follow to a destination, 35

harmonious (hahr-MOH-nee-uhs) *adj.* arranged in an orderly and pleasing way, 103

Hindus (HIHN-dooz) *n. pl.* followers of Hinduism, an ancient religion in India, 34

holocaust (HAHL-uh-kawst) *n.* a great or total destruction of life, 147

hostility (hahs-TIHL-uh-tee) *n.* unfriendly actions, 121

hygiene (HEYE-jeen) *n.* practices designed to keep people healthy and clean, 148

hypocrisy (hih-PAHK-ruh-see) *n.* pretending to be something that one is not, 19

hypothesized (heye-PAHTH-uh-seyezd) *v.* made a theory based on the available facts, 202

illusion (ih-LOO-zhuhn) *n.* an imaginary or misleading appearance, 19, 63

immigrants (IHM-uh-gruhnts) *n. pl.* people who come into a new country, 27

immune system (ihm-YOON SIHS-tuhm) a complex network of cells and chemicals that helps the body fight disease, 210

immutable (ihm-MYOOT-uh-buhl) *adj.* never changing; permanent, 19

imperialism (ihm-PEER-ee-uh-lihz-uhm) *n.* a political system in which a powerful nation controls other nations or colonies, 25

implication (ihm-plih-KAY-shuhn) *n.* something that is shown to have a connection with something else, 26

incognito (ihn-kahg-NEE-toh) *adv.* in disguise, 219

innovator (IHN-uh-vayt-uhr) *n.* a person who creates new products or ideas, 176

insecure (ihn-sih-KYOOR) *adj.* undependable or unreliable, 122

insight (IHN-seyet) *n.* the ability to understand the inner nature of things, 212

intangible (ihn-TAN-juh-buhl) *adj.* not capable of being perceived by the senses, 201

intern (IHN-tuhrn) *n.* a student gaining experience in a job by working with a professional, 92, 220

interpret (ihn-TER-pruht) *v.* to bring out the meaning of; to give one's own idea of, 158

intimidated (ihn-TIHM-uh-dayt-uhd) *adj.* frightened or timid, 92

investigative (ihn-VEHS-tuh-gayt-ihv) *adj.* curious; searching into things, 202

journalist (JER-nuhl-ihst) *n.* a person who gathers, writes, edits, and reports the news, 91

linguistics (lihng-GWIHS-tihks) *n. pl.* the study of language, 9

magnetized (MAG-nuh-teyezd) *v.* made into a magnet, 177

major (MAY-juhr) *n.* the area of study in which a student specializes, 92

mannequins (MAN-ih-kihnz) *n. pl.* models of the human body used by dressmakers, window dressers, and artists, 84

marvels (MAHR-vuhlz) *v.* regards with wonder or surprise, 219

medium (MEE-dee-uhm) *n.* a material or a way of working used by an artist, 66

memorial (muh-MOHR-ee-uhl) *n.* something meant to help people remember people or events, 72

merchant (MUHR-chuhnt) *adj.* having to do with buying and selling goods, 25

mischievous (MIHS-chuh-vuhs) *adj.* teasing; full of tricks and pranks, 193

Moore, Constance (MOHR) U.S. stage and screen actress during the late 1930s through the late 1940s, 92

motive (MOHT-ihv) *n.* intention; the reason for doing something, 194

Muslims (MUZ-luhms) *n. pl.* followers of Islam, the religion of Mohammed, which spread into India from the Arab world, 34

myth (MIHTH) *n.* usually, a traditional story that attempts to explain nature or people; here, it means something that is not true, 7

naturalized (NACH-uhr-uhl-eyezd) *v.* to have become a citizen of a country one was not formerly a citizen of, 19

negotiation (nih-goh-shee-AY-shuhn) *n.* discussing or bargaining to reach an agreement, 102

neurosurgeon (noo-roh-SER-juhn) *n.* a doctor who operates on the brain and other parts of the nervous system, 7

odyssey (AHD-ih-see) *n.* a long wandering or journey, 151

oppression (uh-PREHSH-uhn) *n.* harsh or cruel use of power, 17

ovation (oh-VAY-shuhn) *n.* enthusiastic applause, 128

pelvis (PEHL-vihs) *n.* a basin-shaped bone that supports the middle part of the body, 218

perspective (puhr-SPEHK-tihv) *n.* a person's point of view or understanding, 184, 213

philosophy (fuh-LAHS-uh-fee) *n.* a person's, or a culture's, principles and beliefs, 73

physicist (FIHZ-ih-sihst) *n.* a scientist who studies matter and energy, 194

physics (FIHZ-ihks) *n.* the branch of science that deals with basic properties of matter and energy, 176

playwright (PLAY-reyet) *n.* a person who writes stories to be acted on a stage, 25

poised (POIZD) *adj.* calm; ready, 131

prejudices (PREHJ-uh-dihs-uhz) *n. pl.* judgments or ideas formed before the facts are known, 213

preposterous (prih-PAHS-tuhr-uhs) *adj.* ridiculous, 8

prescribed (prih-SKREYEBD) *adj.* ordered or established by a rule, 83

prestigious (prehs-TIHJ-uhs) *adj.* powerful because of wealth or fame, 121

primary election (PREYE-mehr-ee ee-LEHK-shuhn) an election to choose the candidate who will represent a particular political party in a later election, 184

procrastinating (proh-KRAS-tuh-nayt-ihng) *v.* putting off doing something, 175

prodigy (PRAHD-uh-jee) *n.* an unusually talented person, 128

propaganda (prahp-uh-GAN-duh) *n.* ideas that are intended to influence people's opinions, 120

qualified (KWAHL-ih-feyed) *v.* met requirements, 139

racism (RAY-sihz-uhm) *n.* the idea that one group of people is superior to another; racial prejudice, 25

ransom (RAN-suhm) *n.* the payment of money or agreement to meet some other demand in exchange for a captive person's release, 147

refugee camp (rehf-yoo-GEE KAMP) a temporary living place set up for people who flee their home country for the safety of another country, 120

regime (ruh-ZHEEM) *n.* the time a particular leader is in power, 147

revelation (rehv-uh-LAY-shuhn) *n.* an astonishing find, 210

righteousness (REYE-chuhs-nuhs) *n.* the quality of being morally right or fair, 76

Rodin, Auguste (roh-DAN) French sculptor who lived from 1840–1917; his most famous work is *The Thinker,* 84

romantic (roh-MAN-tihk) *adj.* idealistic; valuing the emotions over reason, 193

rookie (ROOK-ee) *adj.* inexperienced, 83

scholarship (SKAHL-uhr-shihp) *n.* a gift of money or other aid to help a student pay for his or her education, 18

sculpture (SKULP-cher) *n.* the art of carving, welding, or molding wood, stone, metal, or other materials into statues or forms, 63

sequel (SEE-kwuhl) *n.* a story that continues an ealier story, 46

sets (SEHTS) *n. pl.* scenery and objects used to provide a background for a stage play or dance performance, 63

spiral (SPEYE-ruhl) *n.* a design that curves around and around a central point while getting larger or smaller, 66

stabilizing (STAY-buh-leyez-ihng) *v.* showing less change; becoming normal, 218

status (STAT-uhs) *n.* position or rank in relation to others, 94

stereotypes (STEHR-ee-uh-teyeps) *n. pl.* rigid ideas about a person or group that allow for no individual differences, 25

stint (STIHNT) *n.* a specified period of time doing something, 26

studio (STOO-dee-oh) *n.* the working place of a painter, sculptor, or photographer, 65

superstitions (soo-per-STIHSH-uhns) *n. pl.* beliefs based on fear or a lack of knowledge, 37

surnames (SER-naymz) *n. pl.* family names or last names, 139

susceptible (suh-SEHP-tuh-buhl) *adj.* easily influenced or affected by, 204

symbolic (sihm-BAHL-ihk) *adj.* representing or suggesting something else, 66

symphony orchestra (SIHM-fuh-nee OHR-kihs-truh) a large group of musicians who play classical music on string, wind, and percussion instruments, 156

Tamil (TAM-uhl) *n.* a language spoken by many people in South India and Sri Lanka, an island near India, 193

technical (TEHK-nih-kuhl) *adj.* showing the practical skills of science or art, 140

territory (TEHR-uh-tawr-ee) *n.* a part of a country that has some rights, but not as many as a fully recognized part, such as a state, 185

throw pots shape pottery on a potter's wheel, 73

tolerance (TAHL-uhr-uhns) *n.* willingness to respect other people's beliefs and practices, 184

topiary (TOH-pee-air-ee) *n.* the art of trimming and training shrubs into certain shapes, such as animals, 76

trademark (TRAYD-mahrk) *n.* a distinctive quality or feature that identifies a particular person or thing, 103

transfixed (tranz-FIHKST) *adj.* made motionless, 131

treasonous (TREE-zuh-nuhs) *adj.* involving acts that are intended to overthrow the government of a person's own country, 44

undaunted (uhn-DAWNT-ihd) *adj.* not afraid or discouraged, 186

United Nations (UN) an international organization of about 160 countries dedicated to maintaining world peace, 18

valedictorian (val-uh-dihk-TOHR-ee-ahn) *n.* a student, usually the top student in the class, chosen to give a speech at graduation, 219

verbose (vuhr-BOHS) *adj.* wordy, 18

veterans (VEHT-uh-ruhnz) *n. pl.* people who have served in the armed services, 72

virtuoso (ver-choo-OH-soh) *n.* a person performing with great skill, 128

visa (VEE-zuh) *n.* official papers that allow a person to enter or live in a foreign country, 212

vital signs measurements of the activity of the vital organs, such as the heart, brain, and lungs, 218

zestful (ZEHST-ful) *adj.* anything stimulating, exciting, or full of energy, 86

zoology (zoh-AHL-uh-jee) *n.* the study of animals, 202

BIBLIOGRAPHY

Aruego, José

Morey, Janet Nomura and Dunn, Wendy. *Famous Asian Americans*. New York: Cobblehill Books, 1992.

Rockabye Crocodile. New York: Greenwillow, 1988. (illustrated by José Aruego)

Chandrasekhar, Subrahmanyan

Hammond, Allen, ed. *Passion to Know: 20 Profiles in Science*. New York: Charles Scribner's Sons, 1984.

Wali, Kameshwar C. *Chandra: A Biography of S. Chandrasekhar*. Chicago: University of Chicago Press, 1991.

Chung, Connie

Paisner, Daniel. *The Imperfect Mirror: Inside Stories of Television Newswomen*. New York: William Morrow & Co., 1989.

Chang, Helen. "The Prime Time of Connie Chung." *Savvy*, Feb. 1986, pp. 26–29.

Chung, Myung-Whun

Goldsmith, Harris. "Myung-Whun Chung, piano." *High Fidelity*, Feb. 1975, pp. 32–33.

Morey, Janet Nomura and Dunn, Wendy. *Famous Asian Americans*. New York: Cobblehill Books, 1992.

Hwang, David Henry

"Hwang, David Henry." *Current Biography Yearbook 1989*, p. 267.

Hwang, David Henry. *M. Butterfly*. New York: Dutton–NAL, 1989.

Kim, Richard

Kim, Richard. *The Martyred*. New York: Braziller, 1964.

Nathan, P.S. "The Twain." *Publisher's Weekly*, Sept. 2, 1988, p. 60.

Lin, Maya

Coleman, Jonathan. "First She Looks Inward." *Time*, Nov. 6, 1989, pp. 90–94.

Tauber, Peter. "Monument Maker." *New York Times Magazine*, Feb. 24, 1991, pp. 49–55.

Mehta, Ved

Mehta, Ved. "Personal History (I)." *The New Yorker*, Feb. 11, 1985, pp. 45–46.

Mehta, Ved. *Daddyji*. New York: Norton, 1989.

Midori

LeBlanc, Michael L., ed. *Contemporary Musicians: Profiles of the People in Music*, v. 7. Detroit: Gale Research, 1992, pp. 155–57.

Schwartz, K. Robert. "Glissando." *New York Times Magazine*, Mar. 24, 1991, pp. 32–34, 61.

Mink, Patsy Takemoto

Chamberlin, Hope. *A Minority of Members: Women in the U.S. Congress*. New York: Dutton–NAL, 1974.

Moritz, Charles, ed. *Current Biography 1968*, pp. 253–256.

Montero, Juan

Montero, Juan. *Halfway Through: An Autobiography*. Indianapolis, IN: Philippine Heritage Endowment Publications, 1982. Part of the Filipinos in the United States series (no. 1).

Ngor, Haing

Morey, Janet Nomura and Dunn, Wendy. *Famous Asian Americans*. New York: Cobblehill Books, 1992.

Ngor, Haing. *A Cambodian Odyssey*. New York: Macmillan, 1988.

Nguyen, Dustin

Morey, Janet Nomura and Dunn, Wendy. *Famous Asian Americans*. New York: Cobblehill Books, 1992.

Vespa, Mary. "A Survivor of the Fall of Saigon, *21 Jump Street*'s Dustin Nguyen Relives the Ordeal on TV." *People*, Apr. 25, 1988, pp. 105–106.

Noguchi, Constance Tom

Verheyden-Hilliard, Mary Ellen. *Scientist and Puzzle Solver: Constance Tom Noguchi*. Bethesda, MD: Equity Institute, 1985.

Noguchi, Isamu

Esteron, M. and Hochfield, S. "The Courage to Desecrate Emptiness." *ARTnews*, Mar. 1986, pp. 102-109.

Gruen, John. "The Artist Speaks: Isamu Noguchi." *Art in America*, Mar. 1968, pp. 28-31.

Pei, I.M.

Wiseman, Carter. *I.M. Pei: A Profile in American Architecture.* New York: H. N. Abrams, 1990.

Tan, Amy

Lew, Julie. "How Stories Written for Mother Became Amy Tan's Best Seller." *New York Times*, July 4, 1989, p. 23.

Tan, Amy. *The Joy Luck Club.* New York: G. P. Putnam's Sons, 1989.

Tonegawa, Susumu

Marx, Jean L. "Antibody Research Garners Nobel Prize." *Science*, Oct. 23, 1987, pp. 484-485.

Wright, Karen. "Physiology or Medicine." *Scientific American*, Dec. 1987, pp. 45-46.

Uchida, Yoshiko

Commira, Anne, ed. *Something About the Author* Series, v. 53. Gale Research, 1988, pp. 147-156.

Uchida, Yoshiko. *Journey to Topaz.* Berkeley, CA: Creative Arts Books, 1985.

Wang, An

Wang, An. *Lessons: An Autobiography.* Reading, MA: Addison Wesley, 1986.

Moritz, Charles, ed. *Current Biography Yearbook 1987*, pp. 586-590.

Yamaguchi, Kristi

Deford, Frank. "The Jewel of the Winter Games." *Newsweek*, Feb. 10, 1992, pp. 46-47, 50-53.

Graham, Judith, ed. *Current Biography Yearbook 1992*, pp. 56-59.

CAREER RESOURCES

Unit 1: Literature and Drama

These magazines present students' and adult writers' work, and articles that discuss the craft of writing.

The Horn Book (includes book reviews for young people)

Stone Soup (a literary magazine for young people)

Story (a literary magazine for advanced readers)

Writer's Digest (features articles about ways to improve writing and interviews with writers)

Unit 2: Fine Arts and Communication

The following magazines explore the concerns and happenings of the art world.

American Art (profiles American artists)

American Artist (discusses artistic techniques and materials)

Architecture (features prominent architects and their work)

Asian Art (concentrates on Asian artists)

Unit 3: Performing Arts

Browse through these magazines to enter the world of performing artists.

American Theater (covers playwrights, actors and actresses, and directors across the country)

Dance Magazine (for and about dancers)

Rolling Stone (highlights rock and popular music)

Sports Illustrated (covers sports and sports figures)

You might also enjoy this biography about a Chinese American who traveled to Spain to become a bullfighter:

Say, Allen. *El Chino*. Boston: Houghton Mifflin Company, 1990.

Unit 4: The Sciences and Public Service

To learn more about science and health, watch for NOVA specials on public television. These programs discuss scientific breakthroughs and interview scientists. You might also enjoy the following magazines:

American Health (presents news in medicine and health)
Byte (for and about computer programmers)
Discover (news of science)
The Futurist (theories of the future)
Popular Science (the mechanics of scientific instruments)

For up-to-date news on government, politics, and economics around the world, look for the magazines *Newsweek, Time,* and *U.S. News and World Report.* You might also enjoy the biography of the first Asian-born police officer on the Dallas, Texas, police force:

Fiffer, Sharon Slone. *Imagining America: Paul Thai's Journey from the Killing Fields of Cambodia to the Freedom of the USA.* New York: Paragon House, 1991.

INDEX